REAL
UNDERSTAND
THEIR WIVES

© 2003 Ziggy and Friends, Inc./Dist. by Universal Press Syndicate

..o.. I WONDER iF ONE OF THE REASONS WOMEN THINK MEN GET LOST TRYING TO UNDERSTAND THEM..o.

..iS 'CAUSE THEY SAY MEN NEVER STOP TO ASK FOR DIRECTIONS!

DEAR ZIGGY LET'S JUST BE FRIENDS —S.

www.ucomics.com

TOM WILSON & TOM II 8/18

JOHN R. SHARP, M.D.

outskirtspress
DENVER, COLORADO

Contents

Introduction

"I wonder if one of the reasons women think men get lost trying to understand them…is 'cause they say men never stop to ask for directions."
Ziggy and Friends Inc., By Tom Miller

In 1972, I was a 31-year-old physician serving as an Air Force flight surgeon with an F-4E fighter squadron at Ramstein Air Base in Germany. It had been an easy decision to accept the three-year tour of duty with my family in Germany instead of being sent to Thailand alone for a year during the Vietnam War. My wife, Pat, and I had been married for eight years and were truly having the time of our lives. We lived off the base in a small German town and were enjoying learning a new language and a new culture. For a guy who lives for the adrenaline and testosterone rush of maleness, I was working every day with fighter pilots, almost all of whom came to Germany as a follow-on to their 100 missions in Vietnam. These highly motivated men faced danger daily while performing air-intercept alerts on the western border of Eastern Europe. During my tour with these men, I garnered over 150 flight hours as a radar navigator in the "back seat" of a fighter and was accepted as a member of the squadron, thereby mixing my duties as a physician with flying responsibilities in the squadron.

Surprisingly, the toughest part of my job was dealing with pilot buddies who would try to get "the doc" to cure their unhappy wives. This was exemplified one night when a pilot brought his wife to the Emergency Room while I was on shift as the medical officer at the base's small hospital. I had just returned from a three-week deployment with the squadron to the aerial-weapons range in Spain and had observed the behavior of some pilots with the local women, all of whom swarmed around the "fighter jocks." This particular pilot had a philandering reputation, and right away I suspected this was an issue when he and his wife arrived at the ER. As I entered the exam room, I asked the couple what was going on. The pilot said, "Doc, I don't understand my wife and she is making my life unbearable. I love her and you have got to fix her." He then promptly stood up, wryly commenting as he left the room, "Don't let her come home until she is fixed."

Having been trained in internal medicine, emergencies like heart attacks and diabetic coma didn't frighten me at all. But, it was entirely different to be sitting in an exam room with a tearful woman whose frustrated husband had brought her to the flight surgeon to "get fixed" like he'd turn his airplane in for maintenance. I did not have a clue about how to fix her. I suspected that she knew about her husband's reputation, and simply couldn't live with it. He couldn't understand why his behavior—as harmless as it seemed to him—should bother her. After all, he married her, he loved her and "boys will be boys."

As I looked at the pilot's wife in that exam room, my heart went out to her. I knew she was destroyed by all of this. I called my wife, Pat, who found some of the other pilots' wives in the squadron to come to her support. A friend took her in for the night and another later helped bring the couple back together. Eventually, however, the marriage ended in divorce.

❦

I wish I could say that over the next several years I sought opportunities within my practice of medicine to help women whose hearts were breaking because their marriages had died. But I simply tried to be supportive and encouraging while suggesting that they talk with their pastor, counselor or psychiatrist. If a husband came to me wondering how to save his marriage, it was an unusual occurrence and I espoused the philosophy of my father: "Husbands are heads of the household, the Bull of the Woods. Treat your wife with love, help support her in taking care of the kids and do not try to understand her." Because I had been raised in a Christian home, I usually also threw in a comment like, "Divorce isn't really an option, so you need to stick it out."

The words of my flying buddy at the ER continued to haunt me: "I don't understand her. She is making my life unbearable." Many times I did not understand Pat, but we had negotiated a live- together relationship. I thought that probably was the best we could expect.

All of that changed in 1987, and what I learned is the subject of the rest of this book. It took a major event in the life of one of our sons to bring me from a state of being clueless about living as a godly husband to the place where I actively began to search the Christian principles of marriage. Little did I know what God had in mind for my marriage. He was going to walk with me through a tumultuous time that, in the end, would bring my wife, Pat, and me together into a ministry of marriage reconciliation.

As a result of these events in our lives, Pat and I obtained specific Nouthetic counseling training through Dr. William Oswalt and Alpha Omega, Unlimited, and Pat completed a Master's degree in counseling. For the last 20 years we have been blessed to serve in churches doing biblical counseling as a ministry. My experience and study led me to believe that when husbands fail in understanding and love, it is the primary source of marital breakdown. It would be like Jesus failing the church; it would fall apart. I have worked primarily with men who profess a Christian faith, yet are in a marriage crisis. If the man wants to make the marriage work, it will. If he does not want it to work or does not do what it takes to make it work, then it usually does not work, no matter how submissive, helpful, gentle and quiet and spiritual his wife is or how much counseling she obtains. There are exceptions, if course, because occasionally a wife runs off with a biker, or the choir director in spite of a husband who seems genuinely interested in making the marriage work. I will have more to say about this in future chapters when we discuss the idea of men's good intentions but lack of a plan or understanding.

The best place for marital guidance for a man's plan and understanding about marriage, particularly God's design, is in the Bible. In this book I will be using God's design principles; I will relate the rest of my story, as well as some stories of other men whom I have counseled, to help men come to the point where they can not only understand their wives but love them as Christ loved the church.

The book *Real Men Don't Eat Quiche*, by Bruce Feirstein, raised quite a stir of the consciousness of manhood over 25 years ago. (1. Feirstein) I read the book but I had problems with the picture it painted of my gender. It was a satire of dumb men—funny, tongue in cheek, a good read, but not to be taken seriously. The book has become an iconoclastic picture of all that is funny or weird or non-feminine about men.

Since Feirstein's book, there have been many more books about Real Men. I haven't taken the time to read many of them because they all seem to be designed to define masculinity in some way that appears to change a stereotype or open up a wider view of men:

Real Men Have Feelings, Too, by Gary Oliver, PhD
Real Men Cry in the Dark, by Michael Baisden
Real Men Wear Pink, by Dan Werner
Real Men Don't Lay on the Couch All Day, by Dwight C. Walker, Jr.
Real Men Don't Say Splendid, by Michael Gorman

I hear men frequently talking about what real men do or don't do. So I want to use that mindset for men to get it straight about what real men are or are not doing with the women in their lives. The man/woman relationship now has become either cohabitating as long as each is agreeable or one that is broken by divorce. In both my personal and professional counseling experience I have come to believe that men who are doing what is most likely to please her are finding the culturally-correct approach. This requires that a man understand his wife.

I want the term "Understanding Your Wife" to counter what the feminist mind considers the basic inability of men to relate to women.

Men are currently being encouraged to explore their masculinity, sometimes to the detriment of their marriage. In the last ten years a new masculinity has been defined in the church. *Wild at Heart*, by John Eldredge, encourages men to go find their wild adventurous side, and he encourages women to let them go be wild, only to return to sweep the women off their feet. (2. Eldredge) *Why Men Hate Going to Church*, by David Murrow, tells us that the absence of men in the churches has occurred because churches do not cater to masculine life-styles and needs.(3. Murrow) Finally, in his book *No More Christian Nice Guy*, Paul Coughlin wants men to ignore the churches that, following a feminist agenda, are teaching men to be nice, unaggressive, milquetoasts. According to Coughlin, men need to become assertive good guys. (4. Coughlin) These authors de-emphasize the soft, gentle side of men and redefine the primary virtues, which will bring them back not only to church but to success as family men, as virtues characterized by the wildness of Christ as He brawled with the money changers in the Temple or uttered insults to the Pharisees to call them vipers. While I enjoyed reading all these books, there is a subtle message which may not be so good in the long run.

Eldredge, Murrow and Coughlin are simply writing in response to the 50-year-old feminist movement. Their purpose for writing is to remind us that men do not need to feel bad about their masculinity or be defective because we got the wrong message from fathers or our earlier church experiences. These ideas, while pertinent and valuable, don't necessarily translate to marital harmony. Yes, these profound books have advice and discussion about marriage, but they are more focused on the male ego that has been mistreated by their fathers or mothers or the feminist movement. These books encourage men to rise to their masculinity described as adventurous, problem-solving and assertive. Women, according to these writers, need to back off of from making men the brunt of jokes, denying their hearts of adventure, and learn to please them by letting boys be boys. Real men, then, are expected to be adventurous, wild, playing in the mud, less verbal, more focused, task oriented and clueless about women.

Getting in touch with our masculine side, dealing with an absent father, living for the adventure will not bring us back to our wives. I love a great time with men—hunting, hiking, climbing and, as a result of the present men's movement, I even love how we're talking more about the adventures in our lives, and how to live with our wives, and how much they mean to us. But all the guys I talk to still say that they don't understand their wives. So where is living on the wild side getting us?

Oh, I certainly agree that we must understand what has happened to us as men, where our passivity comes from, why we are such adventurous people and why the feminine mind is such a turn-off to us. But to tell us that Christ was all adventure and masculine is a stretch. He, above all else, had the true understanding of the feminine as it related to the masculine. I am certain Christ understood women. I don't want men to simply emulate the glorious return of Christ as a magnificent dose of testosterone on a white horse wielding the sword of judgment. Neither do I define men sacrificing for a wife as a floor mat or passive mule. The suffering-servant picture means we are most like Christ not when we win or lose a fight but when we suffer for righteousness sake. Following our suffering, the beauty of our marriages moves toward unity and reflects Christ's relationship with His church.

I am tired of jokes about men not understanding women. We should not accept the world's view, that we can only love her and not understand her. It is only in understanding her that we can love her. I am sure a man can live with a woman many years, and even consider her his best friend, but still not understand her. The Bible teaches us that if a man doesn't understand his wife he doesn't love her as Christ loved him.

1

The Awakening: Life Alone

To be happy with a man you must understand him a lot and love him a little. To be happy with a woman you must love her a lot, and try not to understand her at all.

Helen Rowland

When, in 1968, we discovered that pelvic scarring from a ruptured ectopic pregnancy kept Pat from bearing children, we adopted our two oldest children. In 1987, Pat and I had been married 23 years and we had three sons. Mike, who was then a senior in high school, was a basketball player. Brett, a sophomore, was a ski racer and pianist. Erik, who was then entering junior high, had been our surprise gift from God when Pat miraculously became pregnant in 1975.

I was a colonel, the commander of a regional U.S. Air Force Hospital with more than 400 people under my command. I had worked hard and served with distinction for more than 15 years and was on track to be a General Officer in the Medical Corps. Our hospital at Pease Air Force Base in Portsmouth, New Hampshire, was a Strategic Air Command base with F-111B fighter/bombers. The base hospital was also the source of medical support whenever George H.W. Bush came to the Bush summer home at Kennebunkport, Maine.

In June, Pat and I were invited to attend a small "intimate" birthday party for Vice President Bush at the home of a large benefactor within the New Hampshire Republican Party. That day Bush announced that he was going to run for president. On the evening national news, while the anchorman was telling the story about the Vice President's birthday party and the announcement, Pat and I had a brief moment of fame when our faces were shown in the reception line by the news cameras. I was not watching the news that night, however, because I had just learned of the events that were going to change my life.

In the middle of all the excitement my radio pager went off, which usually meant that something was amiss. It was my hospital first sergeant. He wanted to meet with me as soon as I returned to base. I asked him if there was a problem with one of our troops. "Well, not exactly, sir; I think we have a problem with your son Brett. I suspect he's been in a bit of trouble; he doesn't know that I know. Sir, he's okay, but I need to talk with you."

"I'll be there in an hour; meet me in my office," I said. Now my mind was running wild. Our second son, Brett, 17 years old, had a wild streak and operated from the position that rules were to be broken. His idea of a good day was either riding his dirt bike on the half pipe or racing with the Whiteface Mountain ski team. I knew he had taken up with some kids I didn't like, and we were in the process of setting limits for him. He had gotten a job as a busboy at the Officer's Club where my first sergeant worked off-duty as the manager. I thought the first sergeant was having trouble with Brett's attitude or some other teenage aberration.

Pat and I got home as quickly as we could, and I went to the hospital. I walked over to my office in the command section of the hospital where the first sergeant was patiently waiting. I was in civilian clothes; he was dressed in uniform. I asked him into the room and motioned him to sit down, but he insisted on standing in front of the desk.

He began to speak, "Sir, I am sorry to have to discuss this with you, but since your son has come to work at the club, I have observed that there are occasional bottles of liquor missing. This morning we discovered that the storage room where the liquor is kept had been broken into. Sir, I think your son is stealing booze from the club."

I swallowed hard. Thoughts raced through my mind, wanting to rush to the defense of my son and deny that he could have anything to do with it. I knew the sergeant was the most trustworthy noncommissioned officer in my command, and he worked daily on discipline issues with the young airmen, many not much older than Brett. His sense of duty and honor was above reproach. He would never tell me this if he were not absolutely certain of his accusation. After discussing his evaluation of the situation, I thanked him profusely for bringing it to my attention and assured him that Brett would no longer be working at the club.

After the first sergeant left my office, I had never felt more alone than at that moment. It was as if the entire plan of my life was floating away. "God," I said, "this is a bad dream—I don't feel close to my son, or my wife. I have this sick feeling of utter failure inside me like a rock."

I went home, broke the news to Pat and then went to our home computer and began looking through some of the files that I knew Brett had access to. I found an order sheet that other students could fill out, with a price list of various bottles of liquor. Over the next few days, through conversations with Brett and his older brother, Mike, in some real face-to-face confrontations, I discovered that Brett had become the primary source of alcohol for many of the students at his school. I spoke with parents who confirmed the situation.

My son was not who I thought he was. I ramped up the discipline and control on Brett. Under pressure to comply with rules and behavior norms, he ran away from home and stayed with a friend. The friend's mother was providing her son and my son with alcohol and marijuana and actually called me on the phone wondering why I had not come to her house to pick up my son. I thanked her for calling me and picked Brett up, determined to place him in a substance abuse treatment program. I was powerless to manage this 17-year-old. He needed to be with someone else to manage him, someone who might be able to get into his head.

The Masculine Meltdown

In his men's seminars, *Men's Fraternity* speaker Robert Lewis discusses the present state of manhood. His thesis is that manhood is in a state of confusion, a considerable "masculine meltdown." His seminars delve into the details of many factors that contribute to this meltdown, characterized by men behaving in a passive manner, failing to take leadership in the home and allowing the woman to be the dominant feature of the home. He notes that most homes now have no male figure in them to influence young boys. Men have thus become disconnected from their fathers, many of whom have abandoned them to single mothers to raise. (5. Lewis)

Lewis notes that 50 percent of today's boys have no father figure in their lives.

After that night with my first sergeant, I certainly did not feel like a father figure.

But wait a minute; it wasn't like that. I was around. I did lead our supper prayer time. I did take Brett to his ski practice and his piano concerts. Yet I had to consider that somewhere, somehow, I had missed a relationship or a discipline with Brett that could have precluded these developments. All of my masculine fatherhood was melting down. Lewis even had me pegged: "Some men," he would note in his seminars, "who are still in the home, have been passive participants, leaving the nurturing to the children's mothers while they perform the hunting and gathering of food." I believed that I was to provide and Pat was to nurture. I was the safety, the support and was the knight in shining armor who rode home each night, exhausted from work, and expecting to be treated like a king.

Like many of my contemporaries, I was focused on what I thought was important for my family—to work hard, get ahead and make money. After all, my father missed some of my athletic events and was usually asleep when I came home at night. As a busy physician and senior officer in the Air Force who was encouraged by all his mentors to climb the promotion ladder, I had a ready-made excuse. "Well, Pat, you will just have to do the best you can, because I need to go see a patient, or the general has called a meeting, or we are getting ready to deploy our troops and I need to see them off." Out the door I would go, leaving chaos to reign at my house.

Additionally, Lewis notes in his seminars that men don't have enough friends. After that night with my first sergeant, loneliness and chaos followed me out the door and entered my heart and mind in a way that would change my life.

I really had no one to talk to. I was too proud to talk with Pat about how I felt, more concerned with myself and what impact Brett's situation might have on my career, not on how she might feel. I knew I didn't have friends, I mean friends like women have friends. Pat spends about an hour a day chatting with her girlfriends. I hate to pick up the phone. Oh, yes, I can enjoy sitting around playing poker, watching Monday night football, belaying one another on a technical rock climb or racing to be the first to climb to the top of the hill. I would even enjoy having lunch with some guys, but I didn't know how to relate to other men on an emotional level. Male conversation is primarily about what we can do that is really cool, better than what another man can do, or that demonstrates my great wisdom, strength, or some other characteristic that is designed to "win."

Lewis also adds that ours is a competitive world, and it remains so until we come to the place that winning isn't necessary for our self-esteem. Try carrying on this competitive one-upmanship in a crowd of women around the office and men will quickly find themselves talking to their coffee cup. Carrying the competitive nature with your children, never letting them even win a checkers game, might produce children who simply give up. After that night with my first sergeant, this wasn't a competition; I was incapable of "winning." I had simply just lost control of my son.

Moreover, Lewis tells attendees at his seminars, men can't relate to their children. Women are acutely aware of when their children are afraid, hurting or sick. Most women usually know every one of their children's teachers and whether the child is having trouble in school. Pat knew all of our son's friends and their parents. I was only vaguely aware that there were little people in our house.

I thought my boys enjoyed being with me on hiking trips, fishing or skiing; that they valued dad's wisdom and maleness. If that were true, why was it that they went to their mother to discuss problems or fears or when they were hurting? Yes, they listened intently when we had our family prayer time and Bible study, when I could impart some of God's wisdom to them, but it was with their mother that they prayed from their heart. It was Pat who had the conversation with them in which each of them gave their hearts to Christ.

After that night with my first sergeant, I realized he knew my son Brett better than I did.

Finally, Lewis indicates in his seminars, men today have lost the lofty vision of manhood. Our prison population is 95 percent male; 90 percent of violent crime is committed by men. Men are abandoning their families at an unprecedented rate and giving up leadership in virtually all areas of society to the point that radical feminism is replacing our previous male-centric society. According to Lewis, our children are learning that men are passive participants in families, the workplace and society. Men are relegated to participating in or watching violent sports, reality TV, looking at women while drinking beer and singing country music about losing their truck, their women and their beer. We have become subjected to a life of futility, enslaved to our corrupt nature.

After that night with my first sergeant, I felt defeated, embarrassed, hurt and trapped by the child whom I loved but did not in the slightest understand. Why did Brett do that?

The Long Road Back

Brett and our family spent 28 months in an adolescent treatment program. He was very resistant and had uncanny skill at running away. While the program was working on Brett, Pat and I were placed face-to-face with our own codependent and dysfunctional behaviors. I was the absent father, and Pat was known as the enabling but atomic mom because she would explode on occasion when situations overwhelmed her. Brett eventually overcame his behavioral dysfunction and became a peer counselor in the rehabilitation program.

Pat and I participated in parent groups, attended Al-Anon, had accountability partners, and gradually our marriage relationship began to improve. There will be more specifics on this growth later in the book. I was still determined to not end up in divorce like many parents of druggy kids that we had met. But I did not believe my marriage was a glory to God. Yes, we were a bit happier; our oldest son, Mike, finished high school and was off to college. After completing the rehab program, Brett was beginning to make his way with more maturity. Pat and I had some skills in anger management or were able to turn away fights, work a 12-step program, assess personal moral inventory and confess our shortcomings. But we were not "one flesh." We didn't have the oneness or unity to deal with this tragedy much less have a ministry together. I had no idea what God's plan for marriage was. I felt as though other people were getting my kids' lives together, but my life was about as lukewarm as an old pizza on the coffee table on a Saturday night.

I'd like to say that everything turned around overnight, but that wouldn't be true. I was still alone in my misery two years later; I did not feel at one with my wife because I was ashamed. I felt like a colossal failure. There were times that I thought about just packing it up and leaving. God would not let that thought stay too long because it has a very lonely feeling with it. My problem was trying to figure out how to think in a different way.

Help Me, I'm Hurting

I just went about my life in a routine fashion without much consideration of my family. I poured myself into my Air Force career. Not a whole lot had changed. Two children were out of the house, our youngest, Erik, was starting high school, and we had moved to Texas.

It really is amazing to me, now when I look back, how much God protected me from my prideful self and worked first in the life of my wife who searched much more diligently than I did for a biblical answer to our marriage.

Pat was still hurting as well and also knew that there must be more that God had in mind for our marriage and our family. A girlfriend, with whom she shared some of our story, introduced her to Dr. Bill Oswalt, a Nouthetic (Biblical) counselor with Alpha Omega, Unlimited. Through diligent work and study with Dr. Oswalt, Pat began to display a quiet, gentle, submissive spirit. She kept asking me questions, pointing out Bible passages that she was learning and encouraging me to meet Dr. Oswalt.

I wasn't keen on doing that. I was having trouble believing that I was in need of some mentoring in my marriage. I was still focused on my work career. But something continued to gnaw at me. I knew Pat was an intelligent woman; she had always studied Scripture and was involved in Bible studies. I was envious of how she studied and trained with Dr. Oswalt. I found myself wondering, "Why was all this happening to me?"

Mike began to flounder in college, and it was apparent that drugs were having a toll on his life as well. No amount of lecturing, teaching, cajoling or discipline would achieve the results I wanted in my sons' lives toward independence. Erik was grouchy with the fact that his mother and I seemed to be "all up-tight" and involved with his two older brothers all the time, with no time for him.

The gnawing intensified. I didn't know where to turn. I think I was just going to stay with my head in the sand. But Pat didn't stand still; she didn't give up. She was following this biblical injunction:

> Likewise you wives, be submissive to your own husbands, that even if some do not obey the word, they, without a word, may be won by the conduct of their wives, when they observe your chaste conduct accompanied by fear (1 Peter 3:1–2, NKJV).

In an Understanding Manner

I was noticing the diminution of anger and control and a new peace that Pat was displaying. I believed it was harmless enough to go to some of Dr. Bill Oswalt's Bible studies and seminars. Being around Bill's teaching caused me to study God's Word, and through Dr. Oswalt's encouragement he gently introduced me to the following:

Likewise you husbands, dwell with them with understanding, giving honor to the wife, as to the weaker vessel, and as being heirs together of the grace of life, that your prayers may not be hindered (1 Peter 3:7, NKJV).

Now, that was the most ridiculous thing I had ever heard. I had been with Pat long enough to know that she thought differently than I did. But I, like every other man I've ever met, believed it was not possible to understand a woman. I thought men do not have the natural emotional connection that women do, and we believe that the woman is a weaker vessel whose job is to submit to her husband and let him rule the family, which means he gets to do pretty much what he wants. My motto was, "If you have a problem, just tell me and I will fix it—that's what I do. But if you want to talk about it, go talk with your girlfriends."

Bill pointed out to me, "Why do you think God has that verse in His Bible?" The obvious answer was that it has to mean something to men, and maybe it wasn't quite as ridiculous as I thought. He continued to work with me by encouraging me to carefully study the subject. I started joining Bill in seminars and even began to team-teach the seminars with him. Since I loved to teach, Bill was putting me in situations that piqued my interest and kept me focusing my study.

I began to change, and as I was beginning to understand this information about marriage relationships, the empty, confused pride within me began to diminish. I learned that the purpose of marriage is to grow in understanding our wives, and the degree to which we experience success in marriage is the degree to which we have understood our wives.

In the latter part of Peter's exhortation to husbands in verse 7, he clearly indicates that our prayer lives will be hindered if we do not understand our wives. That was an eye-opener for me. To think that

God has equated the success of my spiritual life and relationship with Him to the degree to which I understand my wife was a revelation. He gave me my wife as a gift designed to perfect my prayer life with Him. Understanding is defined as: I must gain a high degree of intimacy with the inner workings of my wife and a grasp of her mental thought processes, emotional needs and physical desires before I can expect to have a full relationship with God through prayer.

Peter is telling men that darkness and pain in their marriage relationship hinders their communication with God. The light we are looking for is not just adventure, male problem-solving, masculine church music and assertive behavior. I am a fantastic adventurer. I have always been a dreamer and reached most of my goals. I have not suffered from a "nice guy" disability and can be assertive with the best of men. A befuddled masculine journey and a milquetoast nice guy were not my problems. I just didn't understand the immense joy and power of focusing on the nature and personality and needs of the woman who has miraculously stayed at my side through all these years. I was just alone, and Pat would occasionally tell me that she felt that I really didn't need her. She had it right, too.

I was starting to wonder about whether Pat really grasped what I was struggling with. Did she understand what I was learning? The Bible doesn't have a lot to say about instructing women to understand men. The Bible doesn't command women to understand their husbands because I think most women, by their nature, already understand men in general and their husbands in particular. Women often say to me, "I don't like what he does, or I wish he would do a certain thing," but they usually understand him exactly. They already know that we are motivated by competition, are self-serving, ego-centric, testosterone-controlled, incapable of an emotional attachment, just looking for sex and can only concentrate on the process of conquest.

Real Men Set the Pace of Marriage

What I began to understand more fully, as Bill and I explored who I was, is that I had missed the connection between the relationship I had, or did not have, with Pat and what was going on in the lives of my children. He told me that the most important thing a man can give his children is a solid marriage. The union of a man and his wife is a reflection to the world of Christ's solid relationship with His church. That is the essence of family—one man and one woman so fully devoted to each other that they are simply indistinguishable as individuals. A real man is a father who unconditionally loves his child's mother. What my children wanted to see from their father was how much he was willing to change his worldly view of manhood and demonstrate a sacrificial love for their mother.

The Bible has insight about the union of a man and a woman. I had no idea how much information there was about this in Scripture. Throughout my life, up to that point, I had concluded that the Bible did teach an unconditional love, a binding covenant commitment, that the man was the head and good wives were submissive. That's all I knew. As far as I was concerned, that's all there was. With continued guidance by Dr. Oswalt, and my own study and experiences, I began to understand what a man's relationship with his wife means. I had to grasp the biblical counsel concerning where men and women have come from, where we are now, what makes a woman happy, how she visualizes relationships and how she reacts when she is not in right relationship with her husband. With that information in mind, I could become the man I needed to be.

The Masculinity Movement vs. Marital Harmony

To understand a woman does not impose qualities considered feminine on a man's personality. Some editorialists, such as Brandon O'Brien, writing in *Christianity Today* (April 2008), consider that the masculine movement is trying to impose qualities considered masculine on an image of Jesus, who was seen as soft and feminine for over a hundred years, solely to re-energize the masculine movement. Remember, if somehow we make Christ the model of masculinity, women can't imitate Him. I don't want men to become feminized. I don't want women to become masculinized. Both genders need to be transformed into the "image" of Christ. (6. O'Brien) I desire that men should be what God designed men to be. Men are not simply reduced to brash, offensive, self-reliant, competitive, adventurous or punch-you-in-the-nose cowboys. I am certain Christ understood women

Helen Rowland, an American satirist who lived over a half century ago, said, "When two people decide to get a divorce, it isn't a sign that they don't understand one another, but a sign that they have, at last, begun to." (7. Rowland) She was only parroting what was the mantra of marriage at that time. I don't believe Rowland's quip speaks to all of the truth in marriage. I believe men make the marriage work by understanding their wives, by learning to work with them and by presenting to the world a picture of marriage that reflects Christ's relationship to the church.

A real man understands his wife. He is always in a process that focuses his energy on increasing his knowledge of the feminine. He will not become feminine, or even begin to think feminine. What he is learning are the unique features of his wife and how to dwell with her so that they both grow in relationship. A real man does not whine when his wife fails him, nags him or refuses his advances, because he understands what has brought her to this place and knows what to do next. That information is the subject of subsequent chapters where we will discover the Bible's information about men and their lives and marriages.

2

In The Beginning
The life of relationship

Love seems the swiftest, but it is the slowest of all growths. No man or woman really knows what perfect love is until they have been married a quarter of a century.

Mark Twain

Dr. Willard Harley, in his book *His Needs, Her Needs*, notes that marriages fail because, "Couples fail to make each other happy, or they deliberately make each other unhappy." (8. Harley) I would state such a truth this way, "Men who understand what they bring to marriage today will be better at making it work than those who don't." So learning a bit about how we got to a social structure like we have today seems appropriate since home life was not always like it is now.

Robert Lewis in his book, *Rocking the Roles*, teaches that even the traditional marriage of the first part of the 20th century was a set-up for the marriage crisis of the last third of the century. The working man left the farm or small store in which he worked for the industrial growth of larger businesses. He was gone longer hours and was absent from influence in the home. The women were left at home to nurture the children and to maintain the house. The pursuit of retirement and the life of leisure became the goal of every man, and he needed to rise in the business world to ensure that someday he could retire in comfort. (9. Lewis)

The search for independence, success and retirement eventually led the family to determine that two incomes would be necessary, so the wife went to work in increasing numbers in the 60s and 70s. Women began to demand equal pay for equal work. Traditional men's desk-jobs in mid-level became filled with women. So now not only was the father absent from the home but so was the mother, and a generation of child care, communally-raised children began to grow up. The revolution of feminism was underway. Women wanted equality, opportunity and control of their own lives.

This diversity of roles in the couples, the sexual revolution and a host of other sociologic reasons led to what has become an epidemic of divorce and remarriage with blended families. Since there wasn't a home to link to, many of these children wandered from one parent to another in search of relationships. What they became were disaffected, confused, emotionally-robbed children. Not surprising, as these children grew up they wanted nothing to do with the traditional two-wage-earner, children-forgotten, blended-family model and chose not to enter into long-term marital relationships because they had no basis of intimacy to reflect on. Today they simply live together. Now most couples don't even get married. Nobody commits to anything. A young couple on a first date on a sitcom on cable TV ended with the guy saying, "You know, I really like you; you're beautiful, friendly and really carry a good conversation. Do you want to move in together?" Her retort was a cryptic, "Well, you know, I'm already with someone."

What has happened? As Lewis has written, we have a dual-parent-working home, children in the care of someone else and divorce and blended families. Making someone unhappy seems a lot easier than it used to be. After all, with no commitment we can wake up some morning to discover an empty bed and an empty closet. Besides, there is no reason to work on a relationship; just go find someone else. The kids will go with whichever parent wins the custody judgment or with the mother if she wasn't married.

I am sure that the rise of feminism was multi-factorial. My observation of it over 40 years has been primarily driven by desire for equal pay for equal work. The fatigue generated by working reduced the nurturing role at home. Women determined that they should be equal in all things, which resulted in breaching the traditional male barriers such as service academies, military combat pilots, most of the professions, public service and, now, even the presidency. There have been significant gains that deserve our applause. Only the radical fringe was demeaning to men.

Columnist Kathleen Parker of the *Orlando Sentinel* notes that feminism, which encouraged women to be smart and successful and to be hostile and demeaning to men, has discovered that as a woman was trying to make him be her girlfriend, what's-his-name inevitably lapsed into guy-ness. As the relationship collapsed, she wanted him to disappear. If children were involved, women got custody and men got an invoice. Parker calls the eradication of men and fathers from children's lives feminism's most despicable accomplishment. The women who want men to act like girlfriends, to time their contractions, feed and diaper the baby and go antiquing are remaining longer and longer single. Women want to be in a relationship with guys they can seriously talk to. Unfortunately, a lot of those guys want to be in relationships with women they don't have to talk to. (10. Parker)

It has become a society of women trying to have the man learn to emote and share and stop scratching himself versus a society of men who long for the days of the quiet, submissive woman who stayed home and raised kids and slept with him.

Women Still Want a Real Man

So, feminism was really a hoax, as biographers and historians have discovered about feminist matriarch Betty Friedan. She wrote *The Feminine Mystique* that launched the feminine revolution. According to Alan Wolfe, Friedan's marriage was violent and Friedan clearly knew enough psychology to understand that in America only victims can speak for victims. What she tried to describe did not describe a majority of women. The movement failed to recognize that even smart, successful women also want to be mothers. It's called Nature. Social engineering can no more change that fact than mechanical engineering can change the laws of physics. This means that women need a man. (11. Wolfe)

There is something strange happening now. Maureen Dowd, a *New York Times* columnist, in her book *Are Men Necessary: When Sexes Collide*, notes that men don't want successful working women for wives; they want a woman like Mommy. A University of Michigan study suggests that men going for long-term relationships would rather marry a woman in a subordinate job than a supervisor. So if men want Mommy or women who are not in high powered jobs, what does that say about marriage? One hypothesis from the study was that men really want to minimize the risk of raising offspring who are not their own or even fathering offspring they may not get to raise. (12. Dowd) Today's man really does want some interaction with his children after all.

Dowd and Parker further comment: "Now, in the span of a generation, all that business about equality apparently isn't so appealing to a younger generation of women, who are ever inventive as they seek old ways to attract new men. Today, women have gone back to hunting their quarry with elaborate schemes designed to allow men to think they are the hunters." Even at liberal universities, the percentage of women who take a hyphenated last name when they marry is decreasing in favor of the husband's name. In many cases, women who are looking for husbands in college are doing so because they first and foremost want to be mothers, and marriage is the desirable first step to starting a family. Today's college woman was born after the feminist movements of their mothers' times, and that push for independence might make them feel more inclined to focus on their careers or to wait longer before worrying about having a family. Sarah, a University of Michigan student, says, "But that doesn't mean that it's wrong to be looking for a husband now, especially if having a family is your top priority. Husband-hunting might not be everyone's cup of tea but, in my opinion, the basic message of feminism is the same one that our parents told us when we were children: that we can grow up to be anything we want to be. Whether that's a career woman, a wife and mother or some combination of the two is up to you." (13. Smith)

Learning the Role to Be a Real Man

Did the feminists really think we men wouldn't mind what they were doing? I think men do mind, and what I have devoted my counsel to with men is to return to God's design for marriage. I don't want to confuse men or give them an excuse for their failures by listing what women's problems are. Besides, I am not competent to counsel women about their shortcomings.

Yes, we men have deluded ourselves into thinking we just need a secretary, someone like mother or a quiet submissive woman, with a lot of sex thrown in, and we'll have a marriage. Scott MacGray, a pastor acquaintance of mine, said, "It takes more than country music and hormone surges to make a marriage."

As I have catalogued above, here's a summary of the secular theory: 1) Men leave home to work. 2) Women don't want to live at home. 3) Women want equality in work and home responsibility. 4) Women want guys to relate and be emotive. 5) Guys are guys. 6) Women kick them out or they just walk out because she demands it. 7) Men look for more docile women. 8) Women decide they want to be mothers. 9) Women pretend to be docile.

I don't believe the feminist movement has doomed marriage. On the contrary, I think the failure of men to accept the godly role in marriage produced a catalyst for the feminist movement. So I also have to believe that when we men get it right, the feminists will come home in a hurry.

So here's my theory: 1) Men leave home for work. 2) Men are absent and learn to survive alone. 3) Men don't understand whose job is what in marriage. 4) Men devolve into passivity as situations get more complex, competitive and challenging. 5) Women take over and try to fix everything. 6) Women find men leaving in droves. That's when my fighter pilot friend drops his wife off for me to fix. 7) Women discover they want to be mothers. 8) Men will need to rise to the biblical role.

Earlier I expressed that women are discovering new ways to get the man to find them, and our wives are longing for us to relate to them. Let's look at what you can do to make yourself more pleasing to her.

The apostle Peter wrote about five issues that can go a long way toward starting your journey to understanding these principles.

> *Husbands, likewise, dwell with them with understanding, giving honor to the wife, as to the weaker vessel, and as being heirs together of the grace of life, that your prayers may not be hindered* (1 Peter 3:7, NKJV).

These are the essential elements of what God says women need:

1. We are to dwell with our wife because the woman has a need to be **supported**
2. We are to understand her because she needs to develop an **emotional relationship** with a man.
3. We are to give her praise and honor because our wives deserve **significance**
4. She is a weaker (or delicate) vessel because she needs a man for **security**
5. We are heirs together because of her need for **companionship** in all aspects of her life.

In my experience, most men do not innately learn these principles. That should come as no surprise to us because the way in which we learn how to live with a woman occurs in a rather chaotic fashion. Most of us have either experienced a broken marriage in our parents, our wife's parents or one of our siblings. What we grow up with and learn from our parents' experience is a powerful source of our own views of marriage.

Pat's parents divorced when she was a sophomore in high school. Her father was an alcoholic and, though her mother was a good provider, she was not much of a nurturer. Pat pretty much became the adult child to keep the home in place. My parents lived together until my mother's death in her 70s, and I had a pretty happy youth, or at least I thought I did. Dad owned three funeral homes in southern Colorado and was a deacon in our Baptist church; we affectionately called him "The Bull of the Woods." Mother was left to bend to his desires and plans and to raise six children. Her father was a Southern Baptist minister and he and Grandma lived in or home town during my youth. Dad hired a housekeeper/babysitter; whenever mother had to go to the hospital to get a break from us children, either the housekeeper or my grandmother stepped in. My dad was far from an emotional guy; he simply expected mother to keep it together and get it done, pretty much like what he expected of each of us children. Mom dutifully rose to the occasion, just as each child did. I have three brothers and two sisters, each with great professional success. Each is married with children, and Christian faith runs deep in our family. We looked like a successful family, but there were some storm clouds. At the end of her life my mother was severely depressed and on a lot of prescription drugs, my youngest brother and sister both had been divorced but found wonderful new spouses, and my son was in drug treatment.

What I took into our marriage were three principles:

1. Your wife should never divorce you.
2. Your wife should just keep it together and follow your lead.
3. Your wife should be able to ski.

Now here were the operational principles in Pat's mind when we got married.

1. Find a hard-working, sober man who can make money.
2. Find the kind of man who can be the man your father was not.
3. Find a man to father the children that she would nurture.

Look at these two very different pictures and tell me we were not cruising for a disaster.

In our first 20 years I would have to repeatedly convince Pat that she should not leave me, that divorce was not an option, and that I could change. I was noticing that even my second operational principle and hers were incongruous. I did not intend to be her father, and if she had a problem, it was up to her to fix it. I remember once that I even called the psychiatrist to make the appointment for her. I think I once went along just to show moral support, not ever thinking that the problem was me. After all, I did not come from a broken family.

She did, however, learn to ski with me.

The Creation Story

The other powerful source of influence in marriages is the very different nature of two individuals created male and female by God. It was Dr. Oswalt who began to help me look at our marriage another way. By going back to the Genesis account of creation, I discovered that the account includes the explanation of marriage. So what can we glean from a study of these first chapters of Genesis?

The story of the creation of man and woman in Genesis is fundamental for helping men understand what God has in mind for their relationship with a woman. The man was created first from the dust of the earth, and he was alone. He was given dominion over the animals and was observing, as he named them, that they each had a companion. It is at this point in the account in Genesis that God created the woman. Read Genesis 15:7–25.

I wondered why she was not created out of the dust of the earth like Adam. Pat says that it is because God knew little girls didn't like getting in the dirt and little boys did.

"Why wasn't she created out of thin air?" She said, "I think it is because men could not then accuse them of being airheads."

Seriously, God put Adam to sleep and removed a rib from him from which He fashioned the woman. There must be a really logical explanation why God took Eve out of Adam. The explanation is absolutely profound.

I gather several pieces of information from this surgical operation: 1) Within the original man, there was a complete male and female (Genesis 1:27). 2) The resulting woman produced from a rib was quickly recognized with awe by Adam, who noted, *Finally, here is one like me with bones from my bones and a body from my body* (Gen. 2:23, ERV). 3) Adam knew that he was now missing something that had been taken away from him.

Furthermore the Genesis account next makes it clear that there was a reason for this surgical procedure: (that)... *A man will leave his father and mother and be united to his wife, and they will become one flesh* (Gen. 2:24, NIV).

When this wonderful story is examined in terms of its eternal truths, we understand that man was created first with responsibility to tend the garden, name the animals, and that he was complete in himself with all maleness and femaleness but without companionship. After the surgical procedure, he was given leadership of the woman and he named her. This clearly indicates that everyone needs a head; we do not function very well without it. Man is called to leave and cleave—to leave his own family, cleave to his wife, and the two will become one flesh. I believe this is the completion of the process begun when the surgery was first performed. The return of a man and a woman united in one flesh is the completed expression of the development of a unity. Each is incomplete without the other. The strengths of one complement the other; the weaknesses of one are dependent on the strengths of the other. Finally, the woman was created for man and from man, comparable and suitable. For the glory of man, God made a helpmate suitable for the man from the man. Reuniting with her in a relationship of one flesh is the reason the man is to leave his parents (see Gen. 2:18).

I have to admit that I never quite understood this story in all the years that I had heard it. I had been groomed in the "Bull of the Woods" concept quite well; I did not think I needed a helper (except to take care of the kids while I worked). I certainly did not think in terms of needing an advisor, and it never occurred to me that I was somehow defective in an area that only a woman could help.

I remember muttering one day, after Pat had begun to understand the depth of her helpmate role, "Why are you always nagging me?"

She promptly told me, "Honey, Dr. Oswalt tells me that's my job." I gradually learned that the difference between nagging and encouragement is not in what she is saying but in how fast I understand it and make a change…after all, there is certainly no person more interested in my success than my wife.

∞

"What time are you getting up, John?"

That's how it usually begins. I was asleep. I intended to sleep until I woke up. I didn't need to work today. I didn't want to get up.

"What time is it?" I asked, not even moving from under the gigantic pillow that is half-wrapped around me.

I was now twelve weeks out from my second hip-replacement surgery, and my orthopedist told me that I needed to walk on it more to reduce the last bit of discomfort in my thigh. The trouble is, I do not enjoy the discomfort that is there when I first start out and I never enjoyed walking anyway. I had my first hip replacement surgery 16 months earlier and it still hurt. I want to jog but my doctor says I shouldn't. This morning, it did register with me that I have not jogged in two years. In that same recent two years I have not even been comfortable in climbing up any of Colorado's 14,000-foot peaks with my brother, Tom, an annual week-long excursion we had been doing for almost ten years. So, in my sleepy haze, I figured what I was supposed to be doing was sleeping; I cannot run, I cannot climb mountains, but I can sure sleep.

"It is seven o'clock. Are you going to walk with me?"

Now I have a choice to make. She is either on my side or against me. She either wants me to suffer through an hour's walk to keep her company or she wants to rehabilitate my legs.

"Yeah, I guess so," I say, unwinding from the pillows.

I get up and mutter, "Let the games begin." I stare at the window, not out of it. I don't even notice the golden fall colors of the leaves on the ski mountain. I love to look at the mountain when it is all covered with snow. I am sitting on the bed, making sure I don't internally rotate and possibly dislocate my new hip, trying to decide which route we will walk and how long I will last before I get that tell-tale ache in the lateral thigh that I have grown to expect when the new metal prosthesis in my femur feels like it is rubbing a raw nerve. I first noticed that pain while walking back to the car after skiing fresh powder a few weeks before. I thought God was really good to me in these new hips, because apparently the mechanics of skiing with hips flexed wasn't a problem. It was just walking that was miserable. Even riding my mountain bike didn't bother the prosthesis.

"So why," I thought over Pat's requests, "did I need to walk?"

"If you want to climb Mt. Harvard with Tom, you'd better get going," she said, as she went out the bedroom door.

We were out and walking for several minutes and I was limbering up. But it was not over yet. "Why am I here?" I asked myself, almost afraid to think about ever running again. I reflected a moment about the exhilaration I remembered on reaching the summit of 14,204-foot Crestone Needle eight years earlier and the following eight-hour hike out with a 50-pound pack.

The roadway is flat; the pace is pretty good. Pat has always walked faster than I do, but she seemed even faster today. "What is she trying to do?"

"I sure wish we could put a big bunch of rocks in front of the house to keep all the scoria from the snow plows off our lawn," she said.

I was trying to negotiate staying off the uneven cracks in the road so I wouldn't trip, but I did manage to answer her. "You know, honey, I just can't get excited about buying a bunch of rocks. We'll have to move the sprinkler system and plant a bunch of trees as well, and that's a lot of money." I even put a closing statement into the cutting remarks. "Why on earth would you want a bunch of rocks when all we do each spring is hire someone to rake the scoria out of the yard?"

She became quieter. We just walked in silence. I asked, "What's wrong?" She said, "Nothing."

Now I had another choice. My old way of thinking was telling me, "If I ask what is wrong and you say nothing, I will act like nothing is wrong. I know you are lying, but it is not worth the hassle." I did not want to get into the yard-and-stones deal. It really was a lot of money. Should I challenge her "nothing" comment? I figured she would eventually think of something else to say.

"How is your hip feeling?" she finally asked. I thought about asking her to slow down but my ego wouldn't let me. I wished I was still in bed.

"Well, so far it's fine," I said. I waved to our neighbor as he was setting out the trash barrel.

Pat said, "They just moved in last week and have the cutest little baby boy. She is a good friend of your nurse." I didn't even know they were new neighbors.

I wondered, "How does Pat know all that." It dawned on me that I am clueless.

While I have loved Pat since the day I met her, my growth into unity with her has always been a stuttering two-steps-forward-and-one-step-backward affair. This walk today was not about me; it was about us. She did not have to wake me up; I did not have to get out of bed, and I don't even have to talk to her while we walked. After all, when I was jogging with my buddies in the past, I only kept asking them questions so they would talk too much and use up precious air so I could lead the run home. I thought about that; I thought about how much Pat always touched the lives of our neighbors, how she always invited the neighbors to our house whenever we moved into a new neighborhood. I thought about how she came to the hospital and just sat watching videos with me after my second hip surgery three months before. I concluded that I needed to interact with her, to accept her encouragement, to give her some encouragement.

We were probably 20 minutes into our walk and talking was easier. I explored how she and her sister were feeling about her mother's health at age 90. She wondered with me if I was still enjoying my part-time practice. She explored at which of our favorite restaurants we would eat that night.

"How can she be thinking about supper already? I haven't even eaten breakfast," I mused, as I noticed that the telltale ache in my thigh wasn't there when we passed the bank building as it had been yesterday.

Now I started to notice the bright fall colors of the aspen on the ski-area mountain, Mount Werner. The mountain seemed to be peeking at us between buildings and, as we passed each building, the sun shone brightly on a newer section of the mountain. I saw my favorite skiing run bathed in the morning sun, which also reflected nicely off of Pat's moisture-covered face.

I said, "Don't you just love this time of year; do you ever grow tired of seeing those colors?"

"No," she said, "and the red color is so much brighter this year."

Pat always thinks the reds are more brilliant every year than last year, and she will light up like a candle when we drive around Colorado in the fall to a whole new vista of colors. I think it is because she is so emotional and red is an emotional color. I actually remember only one year in the last ten with bright reds, but I didn't tell her that.

We were nearing the last turn to the house now and I knew I had only a few more moments to recover. I was the selfish one; I had cut off the dialogue earlier. So I finally reached into my growing bag of understanding-your-wife tricks and pulled one out. While mulling over how I was going to present it to her, I noted that my hips did not hurt.

"You're right, the front of the house would look so much better with a nice landscaped earthen berm." I broke into a soft jog and led the way into our yard with a smile in my heart. As I turned, her sweet, sweat-moistened face clearly indicated a smile that let me know she'd heard me.

Here is what Peter had to say about making a woman happy. The five elements I shared earlier in this chapter were:

1. Support
2. An emotional relationship
3. Significance
4. Security
5. Companionship

Support

A man and a woman are to embrace God's design for marriage, that it is a holy union of a man and a woman, destined to follow God's commands, to be fruitful, multiply and populate the earth. A man and a woman are distinct from all other animal life. The singular difference is that man has a capacity for personal relationship. Man is capable of experiencing humanness outside of his own self. We can know there is another person with us, near us or even far from us.

Scientists tell us that animals, no matter how fond they are of their master, do not long for the master when they are apart. Animals do not commit suicide, do not become depressed and are not ever locked in a struggle to design a system where they can appear to be pleasing to a master. Though they do primp and strut around the opposite sex, that activity is hormonal, not emotional. While some species run as pairs, that pattern is a survival instinct, not love or devotion. Moreover, there is no concept of time or space to an animal. Relativity and Chaos Theory are meaningless in the animal world.

The woman God has given me and I are a unique union. We have an intimate relationship. We long for each other. I live in a western mountain community where over 50 percent of homes have pets: dogs, cats, horses, cattle and even llamas. The hospital where I work does not have pictures of doctors or nurses on the walls; there are pictures of "Healing Paws Dogs" and their handlers. Dogs roam the halls of the hospital and wander down the aisles of the grocery store, as well as the waiting room of the barber shop where I go. What do we call our canine pets? "Man's best friend." No matter how late I am coming home, no matter whether I forget to feed him, no matter if I kick the dog when I come home from a long day's work, the dog will lick my face and lie at my feet while I pet him, and he will cuddle up to me on the bed at night. My wife would never do that if I didn't provide for and protect her. If I abuse her, and particularly if I try to cuddle up to her after such behavior, she will more than likely leave me, and she is really my best friend.

The issue here is that a man needs a relationship with a woman that transcends all other relationships. There is a spirituality of connectedness in experiencing an intimate bond with another living entity. While I believe that my schnauzer's delighted attention upon my arrival home provides a boost to my emotional well-being, and perhaps even a boost to my immune system, there is nothing that can replace the furtive glance from my wife when I see her at the end of a week's trip, followed by her hug and kiss.

I believe God always has a gracious intent and, for me, he gave me a woman to demonstrate such intent. He did not give me a schnauzer for such an intent and did not give me brothers, sisters, good friends, significant others, roommates or colleagues for such intent.

Pat is my helper and I, as the helped one, am her partner to carry out God's purpose. We share a common goal, to glorify God through our marriage; we are suitable and compatible by God's design. God uses marriage to meet our needs in the process of focusing on God's greater plan. God purposed through marriage of one man with one woman to produce great value to His kingdom work. Pat and I choose to be of use to God's plans by living as one flesh so we will be of value to His work. Our marriage is our ministry.

Genesis 2:24 states, *a man....shall be joined to his wife, and they shall become one flesh* (NKJV). This is an incredibly profound reality. I say "reality" because when a man marries a woman he should not be focusing on how many ways he can be united with her. I found that I do not want to keep a toolbox of methods to meet my wife's every need. I have already been united.

When a man leaves his father and mother and commits his life to the woman God has presented to him, he is united and they are one flesh. It is a reality; it is what has taken place with the "I do" at the marriage ceremony. They belong to each other, love themselves and each other, become like each other, protect each other and provide for each other. And it is done. His soul, spirit and body are in her and hers in him, just as the original masculine and feminine were one in Adam. This is a profound mystery and it exactly reflects the oneness of Christ and his church.

When I heard that from Dr. Oswalt, I was stunned. The incredibly high calling of marriage means much more than being with someone to be a companion. If that's all it is, I should have just bought a dog. Support means that I am committed to make her life what she needs it to be. Dwelling with a woman is very much like Christ existing with his disciples. To support means to be a buttress against the troubles of life. I am the solid rock when the waves of difficulties descend upon her.

An emotional relationship

Most men I see in counseling explain to me that they are not emotional. I usually assume that means they don't understand why their wife is crying, not that they are unemotional. Emotions are present in all of us; they are powerful in all of us, and they will motivate us to do things or to stop doing things. Don't think that just because a man isn't tearing up in a movie like his wife does that he is not emotional. I find most men were emotional when they saw the World Trade Center collapse or saw their first-born child.

The problem is that men may inhibit expression of emotion because they do not want to appear weak. Appearing strong is very functional thinking if a man is being asked intimidating questions by his boss and he doesn't want to cry. It is very functional if he is on point with his Marine platoon under heavy fire. It is pretty dysfunctional if he is attending the funeral of his mother with dry eyes. It is very dysfunctional if he is inhibited while his wife has just bared a difficult troubling issue in her life and is looking for some evidence that he is actually feeling what she feels.

Don't make the mistake that we have to cry like she is crying in order to demonstrate emotion. We could ask how it feels, express sorrow, sadness, disappointment or whatever word might be appropriate, but don't try to minimize the feeling that she has or simply try to fix the situation. Unless she asks us to fix it, our suggestions are demeaning to her own sense of self-worth. In an emotional moment, we focus on experiencing the feeling and ensure that we know what she is feeling. There will be later time when fixing something might be appropriate.

A young man named Jeremy complained to me once that he was having trouble understanding why his wife always resisted him when he made suggestions. He gave me an example one time when he asked her how her day went. She was working as a carpenter's apprentice and had explained that the truck she was to help unload had become stuck in the mud. He felt compelled to tell her how he would have made sure the load was distributed correctly and to tell her how he would probably redistribute the load in order to facilitate getting the truck out of the mud. This is a classic example of a man who does not understand that his wife wanted an emotional connection and not a solution. He would have gained a lot more if he had asked, "How did you feel about that?" or "What did you think was a way to solve the problem?" rather than to try and fix it. The former approach gives validation to her feelings of frustration about the situation and does not add to the sense of helplessness by pointing out how she did not handle the situation correctly. We really can make more headway by exploring our wife's feelings rather than trying to correct her.

She needs an emotional relationship, and so do we. My wife will get it wherever she can if I don't deliver it. I haven't found it very helpful to say to Pat, "If you want it fixed, ask me; if you want to talk about it, go talk to your sister."

Significance

In order to improve a relationship, we will need to explore what our wives need to maintain their own significance. Praising and honoring her life provides more depth to the relationship than all of the suggestions in the world. In the example noted above, Jeremy really needed to praise his wife's efforts and devotion to her difficult work rather than to act as a problem solver. This is difficult for a man since we are primarily task-oriented and would naturally rather solve a problem than discuss how someone is feeling about it. His wife is a dedicated young woman devoted to the relationship. She desperately needs validation for her commitment to work to financially help the relationship rather than to be in a competitive relationship with her husband who is already a carpenter.

Security

One of the difficult areas for a man to understand is the issue of the woman being a delicate or weaker vessel. To understand this principle that Peter talks about, we need to recognize that delicate is more akin to a beautiful, freshly blooming flower than it is akin to a weaker person of lesser physical capability. Each of us would strive diligently to provide a protective environment for a rare, beautiful flower in order to ensure the continued beauty of such a flower. Jeremy, if his focus was on maintaining the security of his wife, would have questioned her about whether she felt safe and would have acknowledged that she was contributing to the solution of the problem in her work rather than trying to correct what he perceived was a failure to understand how to solve the problem.

Finally, Jeremy was not thinking in a "one flesh" mode and did not express his admiration and gratefulness for his wife's contribution to their family's finances. In his mind they were not heirs together in the gift of life. What she needed from him was recognition of her commitment to their financial stability and recognition of the difficulties she is encountering in her work. What she did not need was a Monday-morning quarterback.

Companionship

I learned from my morning walk with Pat that I needed to rec-ognize her desire for helping me rehabilitate my hips rather than to complain about her spending money. We have been married more than 49 years and you would think I would learn this, but even the most experienced of us can still get it wrong. That day, I received a blessing in my physical wellbeing after I chose to develop a companionship with her and affirm her desire for a pleasant front yard. Her encour-agement to me to continue with my physical exercise produced great improvement in both my physical and emotional wellbeing. I have come to depend upon the benefits of this companionship relationship. I don't understand how it works; I have learned that it does. God's plan chooses us and our helpmate to be one— indissoluble, indistinguish-able and directed for His use.

I know men don't want to go shopping. Shopping is not a sport-ing event and it never will be. Friends think about each other; they do things together and enjoy seeing their friend doing something they like, even when it isn't what they wanted to do. If my wife and I are one, and I want to treat her as well as I treat my own body, then doesn't that mean I have to work on doing what I know is good for her just like I have to work out to take care of my own body? I know it is sometimes hard to shop with a wife. But remember, it is about the companion-ship, not the shoes. So when she says, "Let's go shopping," men think that she already has enough clothes and too many shoes. Men would rather watch the basketball game with her in order to fulfill the com-panionship requirement.

But the other way to look at it is that she wants to present herself to her husband as beautiful and she wants a nice looking home with cool decorations, or she wants to demonstrate her care for a friend by buying a gift, perhaps even buying something for her husband. Some husbands think that their wives are putting too much pressure on them by taking them shopping, hoping they will get the idea and buy her something to show her their love.

I have found some men have difficulty connecting with this idea of sacrificing to meet her needs and have conflicting pictures of what it means. Our natural thinking produces a conflict between what we logically believe and what we need to learn regarding the needs of our wife:

Male leader vs. suffering servant.
Quiet, strong man vs. empathetic friend.
Hard working hero vs. heirs together in life.
Monday-morning quarterback vs. protector
Being together vs. affirming companionship

I know that it was hard for me to think about a woman's emotions, how I should protect her and support her significance and how to learn to think of the feminine. I suffered from a childhood and home where everything seemed to work out well and no one had really big problems. Those experiences caused me to think that something wasn't my problem. So Dr. Oswalt and Pat had a lot of denial and pride in me to work through.

This can be considered a cognitive dissonance which is a characteristic of a man with a double mind. Two things are unable to be rectified to unity or complete relationship in a confused state of mind. I know this is hard; I know it is not the way we men naturally think. I tell my clients that these five are worth memorizing, if for no other reason than that we can begin to change our thinking.

1. Support
2. An emotional relationship
3. Significance
4. Security
5. Companionship

I will have more to say regarding the male sacrifice in Chapter 4. For right now I will use a very common device to help us understand the double-minded thinking about sacrificing for our wives. Just think about a toilet seat. The seat is designed for a double purpose; it can either be up or down, but not both at the same time. Your wife always wants it down. You want it up; at least you should if your aim isn't perfect. The problem is that as far as you are concerned, she needs to learn to work the toilet seat and just put it down if she finds it up. After all, you just pick it up and she doesn't hear us complaining about her leaving it down. I will have more to say about this conundrum in later chapters.

3

Did the Serpent Lift the Seat?
Life within the curse

*God created woman. And boredom did indeed cease from that moment—
but many other things ceased as well.*

Friedrich Nietzsche

Alex was a broken man when he called for an appointment. He was
puzzled why his wife, Judy, had asked him to begin sleeping in the
guest bedroom. He made an appointment with me and the opening
question was, "John, do you think she has already divorced me in her
heart?" He could not understand why she had grown so cold. I have
discovered in my years of counseling that men come to see a counselor
for one of two reasons: 1) their wife has made their appointment with
me a requirement for coming back into the bedroom, or 2) they have
had an affair and are so guilty they need counsel. I call the first type
"The Clueless." The second, I call "The Guilty."

I used to wonder why my own wife was unhappy. Now that I have
figured it out I wonder why every man can't get it. Robert Lewis and
William Hendricks, in their book *Rocking the Roles*, characterize traditional marriage as a mutual tolerance, "nothing more than a contract

that kept two people together in a legal and financial partnership." (9. Lewis) It is characterized by a creeping separateness. Even the best of some long-lived marriages are simply each person developing his or her own interests and lives. They have reared children, purchased homes, approached retirement and yet may wake up some day saying, "Is that all there is?"

Alex and Judy led separate lives for 20 years and, just at the time that his wife wanted more out of the relationship, Alex wasn't willing to change his focus to her from his long-standing self-interest. She wanted a relationship; he wanted sex. It wasn't surprising that since she didn't get the relationship, she wasn't much interested in giving sex.

When Alex started through his story, it sounded pretty much like the pilot 20 years before, only this time when he wanted me to talk to his wife, I very quickly established *Ground Rule Number One*:

"I don't talk to women; the one who needs counseling is you. If you want someone to talk to your wife, then you do it. If you can't, encourage her to talk with her friends or to find a wise older woman to talk to."

Alex didn't know that he was to protect his wife, sanctify her and keep her from harm. No one had taught him that his failure to do that caused her to fail to be the woman God wanted her to be. I didn't need to talk with his wife yet; the one with the problem was in the room in front of me.

I said, "Alex, you are here because you've been kicked out of the bedroom; I really think that we need to assume that the problem might well be something you are doing wrong or, more accurately, something you are not doing right, in order to get to the bottom of this." I even quoted him from the Bible: *Live happily with the woman you love through all the meaningless days of life that God has given you in this world. The wife God gives you is your reward for all your earthly toil* (Eccl. 9: 9, NLT).

Well, Alex didn't buy that analysis. "But she is so angry and cold, so frigid; she can't even talk to me in a civil manner? You know, I understand the phrase in Proverbs that says, *It is better to live alone in the corner of an attic than with a contentious wife in a lovely home* (Prov. 21:9, NLT). The days with my wife are certainly meaningless right now, and she doesn't act like a reward for all my earthly toil."

I knew where he was going with this. Alex believes she committed the first crime, and nothing will dissuade him from that thinking. Then he got to his point and said, "Paul said in 1 Corinthians that the wife should fulfill her marital duty to her husband" (see 1 Cor. 7:3–5). At that moment, I knew Alex was clueless. After two more sessions he admitted he had had an affair and his wife found out about it. He pleaded with me, "But I have a sexual need and she was not meeting it, so I fell to temptation and got it met elsewhere." Now not only was Alex clueless, but he was also guilty.

Genesis and the fall

I presented how to understand what God's desire is for marriage in the first two chapters; now we will explore where the fall of man plays out in the troubles we experience in marriage. The third chapter of Genesis explains what happened to Adam and Eve as well as to Alex and Judy, each a wonderful twosome, so perfectly fitted for each other, so much in love, innocent and designed to complete each other. What happened was that a serpent came along.

Satan is known as *the day star* (Isa. 14:12 NKJV) and was created by God to be a seal of perfection—beautiful, wise and covered with every precious stone. Yet his heart became proud, and he saw himself above all the hosts, and became jealous of God, the only being who possessed more than he had. Satan abused the privilege God gave him and set out to develop a counterfeit kingdom of his own. The tool was deception; he played on man's innocence and, thus, the world fell. He tempted Eve; she was deceived and ate of the forbidden fruit.

OK, so this sounds allegorical, figurative and so very sexist and, "Doesn't it really indicate that the problem is my wife?" Alex timidly tried to challenge where I was going.

Eve was the second in command, like Satan. He presented a plan that was counterfeit. When Eve explained that they were told not to eat of the tree lest they die, Satan countered that they would not surely die, *for God knows that in the day you eat of it your eyes will be opened, and you will be like God, knowing good and evil.* (Gen. 3:5 NKJV).

Now when Eve saw that the tree was good for food, that it was pleasant to the eyes and a tree desirable to make one wise (see Gen. 3:6 NKJV) she took it and ate and shared it with Adam, who also willingly ate of it.

Yes, she fell for the deception, but it was Adam who was there at the same time who did not understand her easily-deceived nature and protect her and himself from the consequence. It is naïve to say that everyone is able to do what is right in his own eyes and then be astonished by the moral chaos that follows. The death of a common morality threatens our very liberty because, without individual con- science, we cannot be held in check except through coercion. Adam's passive failure to stop the bite of the fruit that Eve chose was the proximate cause of the terrible death and separation from God that all mankind experiences.

Alex was now gamely trying to recover his lead in the family and began to bemoan the day he found Judy. "It was the woman whom God gave me," he said, "I just didn't know she would be such a problem."

I said to him, "You know, when Adam was confronted, that was the same excuse he tried to give God. But he was still handed a conse- quence along with all the rest of us men. You married her but you did not protect her; she has been unkind to you only because you weren't there for her." He did not like that at all, so I went back to the Genesis account.

After Adam and Eve had partaken of the fruit, the Lord God was walking in the garden in the cool of the day, and the man and the woman hid from Him. The Lord called out to Adam, asking where he was. Hiding among the trees, Adam spoke up with a rather feeble excuse, explaining to the Lord that he hid because he discovered that he was naked.

Now it's time for *Ground Rule Number Two*: we can't hide from

God. He's going to change us and we'll be miserable until we change. It is clear to me that God knew where Adam was and what Adam had done. He wasn't looking for Adam, who was hiding; He was expecting to confront Adam with his sin. You see, when we sin we have a sense of guilt and shame and lose fellowship with God; we ignore the fact that He is there; we cut off the communication. God wouldn't let Adam get away with that any more than I believed I should let Alex get away with his sin. Alex had just told me that he was banned from his bedroom by his wife and was hiding his sins from God and he wasn't being particularly truthful with me. I knew there had to be a primary failure of Alex, perhaps even an affair that had turned the tide. In my experience, it is commonly the discovery of an affair that closes the bedroom door. Judy knew it and was putting the pressure on Alex, who was now openly naked in front of God and ashamed.

The next response from Alex was as predictable as Adam's response when the Lord asked Adam who had told him that he was naked. God asked him if he had eaten from the forbidden fruit.

Alex said, "That woman I married, she always picks on me; she always has a headache and isn't much fun in bed. So I had an unmet physical desire. When I was with another woman, well, one thing led to another."

When we sin we blame others and do not accept the responsibility for our sin. So how does this happen? Why can't men like Alex see this coming? It seems too simple to say that it was the fall of man and our sin nature that does it. That is too shallow, too fundamental, and doesn't lead to insight. At least that was how Alex processed it. He truly believed in his heart that when his wife became less sexually interested, his inner fire needed to be fed somewhere else.

The Curse

If we explore what happens next in the Genesis account, we discover further insight about our sin nature. First, God cursed the serpent. Satan was eternally doomed for his choices. Next, God turned to the woman and told her that she would experience pain in childbirth and that, when she is operating independently of her husband, her desire would be to control him and to usurp his headship. The Hebrew word translated desire is *teshuwqah* and in this verse it is not a pleasant desire, but an overflowing or running over like a river stretching out to exceed its banks. It is the same word used in other places in the Old Testament for characterizing sin, lying in wait to run over us (See Gen. 4:7 , NKJV). A woman left unprotected, as Eve was, will often try to run over her husband. Further, the Lord told the woman that in spite of her trying to rule, her husband would continue to rule over her. The more easily-deceived woman would, in the end, fail to usurp the man's role.

Alex lit up again, I am sure because he thought he would prevail and win the day. "At least you do agree with me that her nagging is a reflection of her sin, don't you?"

I had to admit that I agreed with him, but I asked him, "The question we have to consider here is, what was the cause of her lapsing into her controlling, nagging mode? Was it something over which you as her husband had some responsibility?"

He was struggling to think outside the box of male dominance he had observed from the family of his youth. He told me his father and mother had a marriage characterized by the absolute rule of his father, best considered a powerful, wealthy man who had no sense of relationships, either with his mother or with Alex. As a young boy Alex had been sent away to boarding school. I suppose it was a real stretch for him to hear that God held him responsible for his wife's emotional satisfaction. This information was giving him trouble.

"Alex," I leaned toward him and continued, "are you responsible for your wife's emotional and sexual satisfaction, for her protection and her security, or does she get that from somewhere else?"

His eyes indicated that I had asked him a question with a significant risk if answered in any way but the affirmative, yet his body was moving sideways to get away from the implication. What he would do with this question would give me a great deal of insight into whether he understood and could save his marriage.

To think he was responsible for the intimacy satisfaction in his wife was a thought for which he wasn't ready. He was hoping a man counselor would be telling him how to change his wife; every time I brought him back to himself, he would stiffen up like a sail in the wind, blowing him where he didn't want to go. But I didn't want to go there with Alex, and his answer to the question let me know we had a lot to do yet for him to understand.

"I don't think she even wants sex anymore and probably never has; how can I meet her needs in that situation?" he pleaded.

I said to Alex, "You asked me how you could meet her needs. That is the question which will begin your transformation."

So here's the point. Irwin McManus, the pastor of Mosaic Church in Los Angeles, says that "the measure of spiritual maturity is the time it takes to go from hearing God's word to doing it."

Many men have a limited idea about what contributes to a woman's sexual satisfaction. Their only frame of reference is their own sexual fantasies and the current level of testosterone in their bloodstream. Usually their own experience, limited by what they may see on the television series, *Sex and the City*, is that her satisfaction is tied to the same physical experience that brings a man satisfaction.

To a woman, sexuality is intricately woven with intimacy, an intricate, delicate, soft, emotional experience that dreams, touches, feels and talks about attention. It is enlivened with her husband's devotion, sacrifice, protection, the power of security and the explosive pleasure of seeing, feeling and knowing she is the total focus of his presence. The more he is able to convince her that what he is doing is exclusively to pleasure her to the exclusion of everything else, including his own pleasure, the more she will be satisfied. I will cover sexuality in more detail in Chapter Ten, but Alex had brought it up early. The issue of sexual dysfunction that he was experiencing was going to be my entry into attempting to change the way he looked at his wife.

Before our session ended, I wanted to finish the discussion about the curse that the Lord placed on Adam's head for his passiveness. To Adam He said, *Cursed is the ground for your sake; in toil you shall eat of it all the days of your life. Both thorns and thistle it shall bring forth for you... In the sweat of your face you shall eat bread till you return to the ground, for out of it you were taken; and to dust you shall return* (Gen. 3:17–19, NKJV). After clothing them, God then rather unceremoniously cast both Adam and Eve out of the garden.

Now, in order to make the rest of their lives work, the man and the woman were interdependent upon God and each other. Adam was still the head of the family, and his choice of the name for Eve was confirmed in the Genesis account after the falling from grace. The trip out of the garden did not change the relationship of man to woman, or the roles of responsibility for the man as the leader of the unit. They would have to learn submission to God. Alex and Judy are doomed like Adam and Eve, save for the grace or God's power within them and the sacrifice of Jesus Christ.

Man: Unique Spiritual Leader

The Genesis story tells us that God's design for the social order was that the masculine, male Adam was created by God with a unique social and spiritual leadership calling. His difference is not just physical, but in his calling and his creation as a man.

Robert Lewis characterizes the creation of men in terms of three concepts:

1. Men are created with a **will to obey**. The world is absolutely immoral. Absolute values exist and the commands of God are liberating, not restricting. Moral values are benefits not burdens.
2. Men must have a **work to do**. Labor is painful and frustrating, but what enriches it is the labor's relationship to God. It must have a transcendent cause.
3. A man needs a **woman to love**. When a man fails to honor a woman, his own honor must be dead. It is the man's role to care for the woman, and that isn't chauvinism.

"Alex," I said, "God's Word tells us that you must understand the feminine nature, that you must see Judy as an extension of yourself, the person God has given to you to honor and protect as a delicate flower, and that she shares everything with you as a single unit in God's grace." He now had heard that he and his wife were interdependent and that the failure of his sexual satisfaction was the result of his failure as a man.

Then I really started to squeeze him: I said, "I know what Paul said about depriving each other of sexual intimacy, but you have not been interdependent. You can't expect her to give you authority over her body if you have not done the same thing with her. You must not have been pleasing her intimately, so what you have now is nothing."

The husband should not deprive his wife of sexual intimacy which is her right as a married woman, nor should the wife deprive her husband. The wife gives authority over her body to her husband, and the husband also gives authority over his body to his wife (1 Cor. 7:3–4, NLT).

Alex did not like that. He stopped coming to see me for a while. I discovered that men who have had an affair looking for more exciting sex have a real problem believing the problem is theirs. It is called denial. Alex, like Adam, was now struggling with thorns, thistles and sweat with increasing difficulty. I really wanted Alex to learn what I had learned, that he was responsible for the state of his marriage. He was the leader; the reality was that when he failed to lead, failed to have a transcendent work in the relationship and did not see his wife as the other half of himself, he was living the curse from the fall and his wife was usurping his role. Living life in the passive, painful struggle of the consequence of the curse is profoundly unpleasant for the man, and appears absolutely hopeless.

Understanding the hopelessness that lives with a distraught couple who are reacting from their curse should be contrasted with how Christ elevates marriage in the New Testament concept. In the Old Testament accounts of creation and the first marriage, we see only the chronology of God's progressive revelation of His grace to man and the continual struggles to accept Jehovah God by the children of Israel. Alex was vacillating between serving God and serving his flesh, just like the Israelites. He had been given the Law, God's design for marriage, but he needed to understand that this the age of grace and the filling of the Holy Spirit of all believers is presented in the New Testament, where our story must move.

If we have only human understanding, and not a spiritual dimension, we are oppressed by the Law, and are not only guilty but ignorant about what to do. Therefore the desires of the flesh overcome us. Thinking first about our wife seems nice, but without the power of the Holy Spirit to guide us, thinking of her continues to be an exercise in futility.

We Christians must strive to think and act in a spiritual realm of truth. It is not complicated. I still fail to continually understand my wife and sometimes the more I try, the more I seem to fail. Every day I understand the consequence of Adam's fall. Understanding my wife is hard work; it is toil, not always pleasant, exposes me to frustration and lays open my selfishness before God in an often painful way.

Alex felt pretty hopeless now; he had to be thinking that I thought the entire problem was his. Well, I did. After all, he is the one who came to see me. Remember Ground Rule Number One: The person in counseling with the problem is the one in the room, not the one outside the room.

I continued to see Alex periodically. I think he really wanted to make his marriage work, but he just didn't understand that sacrificing for his wife was his only choice. That is the lesson of the New Testament. Sacrifice is the answer to the curse.

His relationship was dying and he was sitting by, wondering what had happened. In the analogy of the toilet seat that we used in the last chapter, Alex was wondering why the toilet seat was not always up where he wanted it. Caring for his wife at this time was an anomaly he couldn't grasp. It was like he was saying to me, "Why does she always leave the toilet seat down?" It just didn't seem possible for him to understand that the condition of the toilet seat was his responsibility.

Real men understand their wives. Real men leave the toilet seat down. I mean, after all, as far as she is concerned, the moveable lid is useless; she never moves it. But Alex is still thinking, "She is a big girl. If it's up, she can put it down."

Adam was passive, not protecting Eve. The serpent tempted Eve. Adam paid with being challenged with hard work; Eve paid with having to live under Adam's leadership in spite of trying to take over. Alex never remembers to put the toilet lid down. Judy is always putting it down and leaving it down. She wants to nail it down.

Alex never did figure it out and is on his second marriage now. He was wounded by the past and could not get beyond it. Some warriors never do. In the next chapter I will talk about how to survive our wounds, not wallow with the sorrows still in us. It won't be easy, because warriors expect to sacrifice but they also have to get beyond the wound.

4

Wounded Warrior
The life of male sacrifice

A man who will not lie to a woman has very little consideration for
her feelings.

Olin Miller

Men will be wounded; actually most already have been wounded. We
have already learned that we won't always win, that there is another guy
who really can do it better than us. Some men may have suffered actual
physical wounds from a warrior's duties. Others of us have suffered
from not meeting our own expectations in competition or combat or
our profession in the world; some of us have a broken marriage or
broken relationships with our children or siblings. If we haven't been
already, each of us will be wounded. Somewhere we will fail.

The filling of the Holy Spirit is the only way to solve the pain when
we come face to face with a failed marriage. There is no way to gather
the forces of will power, determination, brute strength or finesse in
one place to make us into perfect husbands. Our nature that has led
to a marriage failure makes us watch the football game and ignore our
wives while they are asking us what we want for dinner, or just remain

silent when asked how we felt about our son's grades. We'll cringe when we know we have to talk to her about her sick mother. We don't even understand what she's crying about when we want to roll over and go to sleep after sex. We don't understand why she worries when we go hunting with three high powered rifles, two decks of cards and three cases of beer.

What now follows is a discovery that a failure in a marriage needs to be dealt with in the same sense of action and purpose as for any other dangerous or competitive activity.

∽∂⌀

In 1972, I got my first international ski racing experience. I qualified to be on the U.S. Air Force Ski Team at the NATO ski meet in Livigno, Italy. I had been skiing since I was eight years old and had finished in the top five three years in a row in the Air Force championships in Garmisch, Germany. Military teams from England, Germany, Italy and Spain were in the event and it would include a downhill on the same Italian course used in the World Cup skiing events. Naturally, I was pretty excited at this opportunity.

Downhill racing is the most dangerous of the skiing races and the most popular and legendary of the Winter Olympic events. It is the only alpine skiing event where a skier actually gets to practice-run the course on which he will run the race. Helmets and downhill suits were a requirement. I moved into the starting gate for my first of two practice runs full of all the adrenaline a 30-year-old male can muster. Pat and our son Mike stood at the bottom anxiously awaiting my rush through the course. I don't think she was as excited as I was.

I don't know what happened. I have heard only from some of my teammates that the crash was spectacular, a high-speed carom off a jump and the failure to negotiate a sharp left turn. I woke up plastered against a hay bale with both skis, my poles, helmet and goggles scattered. I don't even remember the crash.

I was able to get up, refused the assistance of the ski patrol, collected my equipment and skied gingerly down the course. At the bottom, I spied Pat and it looked like her hair was on fire. She walked quietly up to me and first asked me if I was all right. Assuring her that it was only my pride that was injured, she loudly spoke a pronouncement in front of everyone. There was a beautiful calmness in her voice, with a firmness that melted my heart. "John," she said, "Mike and I are going home if you think you are going to do that again tomorrow. I did not marry you to be a widow. You have me, your family and a medical career to think about."

Now I had a choice to make. Did I think the race or my wife would define meaning in my life? Sure, I had learned something about the course; I knew where I needed to be cautious. I had gained knowledge about my capabilities on the snow and where my edge was, but I also learned that the person God gave me was appealing to a relationship and not a macho event to define our lives together. It was like she was saying, "John, your character and leadership, who you are to me and your children, is not bound up in your physical prowess in a ski race. I want you and me to live a long time together."

I bagged the race the next day. Yes, I skied down the course, but I put on a very thick parka and stood up for wind resistance to slow me down. I think that was the right decision. So did Pat.

It was 15 years later that Dr. Oswalt helped me understand more about what the Bible had to say about that kind of incident.

Husbands, love your wives, just as Christ also loved the church and gave Himself for it, that he might sanctify and cleanse it with the washing of water by the word, that He might present it to Himself a glorious church, not having spot, or wrinkle or any such thing, but that it should be holy and without blemish. So husbands ought to love their own wives as their own bodies; he who loves his wife loves himself. For no one ever hated his own flesh, but nourishes and cherishes it, just as the Lord does the church (Ephesians 5:25–29, (NKJV).

Robert Lewis characterizes men in their fleshly pursuits as passive, irresponsible, without a higher purpose and living for the moment. (5. Lewis) I think it's the hormones. Maybe it's in the genes. Why would thousands of men line themselves up on two sides at Gettysburg, Pennsylvania, in 1863 and begin one of the bloodiest battles in history—in defense of what, for the preservation of what? Is that passivity? Is it without a higher purpose? No, of course not. The sacrifices of those Union soldiers for the higher purpose of maintaining a United States was a most significant higher calling in America's history. We could have become two nations divided. We men are very capable and driven under certain circumstances that involve competition and conquest, so we are not in all things passive, irresponsible and without purpose.

And yet, men rarely experience the higher calling of devotion to a marriage with the same self-sacrifice that characterizes the downhill skier or military warrior. I learned problem solving from my father. I learned how to play linebacker from Coach Corky Lyons and went with my football team to the state high school playoffs. I learned how war was waged from a year's study in the Air Force War College. Men learn what it means to fight for what they believe and to never give up. But nobody, and I mean no one, taught me how to love my wife as God had designed it. My sons were now nearly grown men in 1987 and I had not even taught my own sons. Where in the world was I going to learn what to do with my wife?

One weekend, in 2002, our son Erik asked me to go with him while he ran his first skier-cross race at Vail, Colorado. He had developed into an incredible skier, racing in New Hampshire and New York in his youth. This would be his first big meet. He was 24, full of all the vigor of youth and the brains to go with it. As we rode up the lift along the racecourse, which is run in group starts of four racers, I observed the undulating, wildly turning course. I flashed back to my experience in Italy and quickly put it out of my mind. This would be enjoyable. After all, I wasn't going to subject myself to the chaos I saw.

I skied down the side of the course to an area beside a rolling section with a track that fell away from the hill. Erik knew he would need to maintain contact with the snow to make the turn. Then he was off with three others. "Wow," I thought, "They are really moving." As he crested the hill, he sailed airborne past me and disappeared behind the hump. I heard a groan come from the spectators who could see his landing. The other three quickly came into view without Erik. I skied down below the hump and saw him sitting on the snow, skis, helmet and poles off, with a ski patrolman running to where he sat. He couldn't remember where we were for a few seconds and agreed to a ride down on a toboggan. At the bottom, he was feeling fine with a slight headache, but couldn't remember what happened. He wanted to go back up for his second practice run.

This was a very teachable moment. I insisted that if he wanted to make another run, he would have to find another way home because I wasn't going to watch. I even threw in some medical advice about the dangers of two concussions in one day. Then, for the clincher, I shared my Italian experience. He agreed to go home.

About an hour later, in the car, I asked him, "How many times have you done that skier-cross stuff?"

He said, "That was my first time; I think I'll give it up."

I was happy; it did appear he had the capacity to learn. Then I realized that I was not teaching him what I should about life. I already knew there was great risk to adrenaline burning, high- speed skiing and he thought he was invincible, just like me.

As Christ Loved the Church

I have observed from the men I counsel that discovering the sacrificial part of the marriage relationship is not very much fun and brings a sense of despair. The priority relationship is marriage, and marriage is about God, not two people. The apostle Paul encourages men to follow Christ as He gave himself. Gave for what? To sacrifice means to give up something to gain a greater good. Our son Erik was learning that, but would he learn what that meant with a woman.

So I explain it to clients this way: picture God viewing His creation and placing two people together in the way He placed Christ in our midst. Christ came that we all might be saved from our sins. His every thought, action and word was directed at how He was to establish His church, His people, on a higher plane of relationship with Him. Christ and human kind were placed together, the Word of God—His plan, revelation, guidance—was mixed in, and Christ gave up His life that we could live ours. Christ sacrificed because He first loved us. He did not wait until we loved Him. In so giving up His life, we have no blemish in God's sight. Christ took the heat for our sin and as a result we were seen as set apart and without blemish.

A man named Carlos went through his young male adulthood with few friends. He was always doing the right things, never messed up, or around, and avoided all appearances of evil, sensuality or the brutishness of some males. He was every mother's son and a perfectionist in every way. He had only two dates before he graduated from college. He loved God and continually meditated and studied His Word. But he had no helpmate. He became rather fixed in his ways and gained a certain amount of self-righteousness. One of his friends even told him that he needed to find a wife so he wouldn't spend his life alone.

Well, he finally married a delightful woman but he never understood her and didn't depend on her and tried always to make her into something she wasn't. When asked about their troubles during one of our counseling sessions, he would answer, "She just isn't spiritual enough and is too much into the world; she spends too much money and always wants nice clothes and cars." He liked to hunt and enjoyed being alone; she couldn't imagine why anyone would want to kill an animal and she always wanted to talk. Carlos didn't rise to the occasion. He would not complete the remodeling of their home for five years. His wife simply withdrew.

Carlos was wounded from his past: his pride, loneliness, rejection by his father and lack of intimacy. His wife had been abused by a relative as a teenager. As their children grew older they sensed that their parents weren't together, since they had begun to sleep in separate rooms. Carlos couldn't relate to them and they gradually grew into sullen teenagers or withdrew like their mother. Fights would occasionally break out, usually around money, sex, the children's behavior, and solutions were short lived. Carlos simply couldn't be consistent; passivity was the route he took. He finally was forced to put away his armor, no longer able or committed to the fight, wounded beyond his own power to recover, transformed into a desperate, quiet and lonely man.

She gradually withdrew, separation was negotiated, and eventually they divorced. He sought solace in spiritual meditation, seeking a higher plane of living; she tried to keep the remaining children comfortable but didn't know how to explain why their father was gone.

Carlos will probably spend the rest of his life alone and she will find a group of women who have experienced similar heartbreaks, but she probably won't spend the rest of her life alone. The children will move back and forth between both parents; grandchildren will grow up wondering why grandma and grandpa don't live in the same place or, worse yet, they might not even know who their grandparents are.

But there is hope for the wounded warrior. God has provided a manual for marriage. Paul's words in Ephesians explain the commitment to marriage in terms of a man loving his wife, nourishing and cherishing her the way he nourishes and cherishes his body. Peter's words in 1 Peter 3:7 indicate that a man must understand his wife, live with her in an understanding manner or dwell with her according to knowledge.

Joel Davisson, in his book *The Man of Her Dreams, The Woman of His*, explains that the marriage manual is written on a wife's heart and the only way to become the husband that our wife needs is to read and follow the manual in her heart. In fact, the only way to become the man God intends us to be is to become the husband our wives need us to be. (14. Davisson)

Men need to learn that loving a woman is *the higher calling*.

Loved Their Wives as Their Own Bodies

Understanding his wife's inner person, how she thinks, what she was created for, how she fits together with him and what their roles of mutual submission and sacrifice are is the very task that faces every man. Let's take a careful look at what this means.

A woman is created to complete her husband; she is the perfect person given to him by God to mold him into the man God wants. He must seek to know what she needs because they are specific and unique to her and they are custom made for him to deal with. There are few universal rules in these situations because what he is trying to do is to knit a unique relationship.

John Eldredge, in his book *Wild at Heart*, notes that most men marry for safety. They choose a woman who will make them feel like a man but not really challenge them to be one. We know in our guts that we are never enough for our wives. So what do we do? We offer what we have. We move toward her. (2. Eldredge)

"But, what if it doesn't work?" That's the wrong question. What were we expecting to work, that she would validate our manhood, come tenderly into our arms and make us feel safe again? If she is the report card of our strength, then we'll ultimately get an F. That's not why we love her, to get a good grade. We love her because that's what we are made to do; that's what a real man does. (2. Eldredge)

When the Bible tells us to love her as we love our own body, here's what I think this means: Men love their own wildness, adventure, skills in doing tasks and their competitive spirit. Loving her means we also must love gentleness, quiet spirits, tears and mercy.

Let's Re-think How to Respond to Your Wife

Here is an exercise in how to feed and care for your wife. Picture the situations as expressed in these comments that I hear frequently from men:

"My wife always wants to spend money."
"She says she doesn't get enough time with me."
"She always wants to pick out the movie, and some of them I don't like."
"The kids are always going to her for advice, and not to me."
"She wants me to sit and watch TV with her."
"She is really bitchy during her 'monthly time.' I just stay out of the way."

Probably most men have thought some of these things about their wives at some time or other. It may be helpful to look at ways to think about each of the issues that focus on how an understanding husband might respond.

God gave a wife to be her husband's helpmate. There is no other person in the world more interested in a man's well-being than his wife. God gives us difficulties to discipline us and mold us into the men we should be. By listening and learning from our wives, we can learn gentleness, compassion, self-denial, attentiveness, love, caring, longsuffering and patience.

My wife always wants to spend money.

"You know, I really am pretty much of a tightwad; I don't enjoy the blessings that come from our money. Thank You, God, for pointing out that I need better financial planning and more discussion with my wife about money."

She says she doesn't get enough time with me.

"My goodness, God, how can I think that spending time bowling with the guys is better for me than being with my wife? The guys only want to beat me and make me pay for the beer."

She always wants to pick out the movie, and some of them I don't like.

"Actually, I really enjoyed that chick-flick. My wife helped me see that I really do have feelings about women who are struggling with broken families."

The kids are always going to her for advice, and not to me.

"It really struck me when she helped me understand that I was provoking my children to anger by not answering their questions or not trusting them to be responsible. No wonder they don't come to me."

She wants me to sit and watch TV with her.

"This is a hard one, but I have learned that she can be more relaxed and share her feelings with me when she's watching those Lifetime shows."

She is really bitchy during her "monthly time." I just stay out of the way.

"Wow, her attitude and emotional labiality during her monthly time can be a real opportunity for me to encourage her. Amazingly, I can find a lot of projects for me to work on myself as a result of the things she says when her guard is down, things that she just stuffs the rest of the month."

Do those answers make us feel funny, kind of unreal, a bit too touchy-feely and less of a bull of the woods?

What Am I Sacrificing?

Some men can't make this feeling adjustment because of the misconceptions they bring to their marriages. Consider that the failure to understand your wife is due to one or all of the following character descriptions. I have included a code word that some of my clients' wives find as useful reminders when they observe it in their husbands:

What I need to sacrifice or give up	Code word
Insecurity about masculinity	Bully
Desire to control all situations	Control Freak
Attachment to the physical	Druggy
Unrealistic personal expectations	White Knight
Ignorance	Dumbo
A seared, guilty conscience	Nixon
People pleaser	Co-dependent
Thinking he has all the answers	President

If the man has security issues, a controlling personality, unrealistic expectations and a need to be a people pleaser, he will need to work out those issues. That calls for a change from old ways of thinking and for an aggressive approach to seeking to be healed from some of these issues. Just as a sports star must take time off from his team's games in order to heal, warriors have to tend to their wounds and be healed before they can think fast enough to give some of the proposed re-thought responses to a woman, as discussed above.

Robert Lewis speaks to the fact that real men will reject passivity, like the passivity which characterized Adam as he stood by and let the serpent destroy the joy of the garden. Like the passivity of Alex when his wife really needed his affection and an emotional understanding. Real men accept responsibility, like taking charge of their family or dealing with addiction or co-dependency issues. Real men lead coura-geously, like choosing to lead their family away from self-gratification and toward a ministry in the family of God. Real men expect the great-er reward that comes with completion of their lives devoted to God's will and the wonderful fulfillment of the woman given to them to sanctify. (5. Lewis)

John Eldredge writes that the masculine journey takes a man away from the woman so that he might return to her. He goes to find his strength; he returns to offer it to her. She needs to know he will fight for her and that she is lovely. The number-one problem between men and their women is that we men, when asked to truly fight for her, hesitate. We are still seeking to save ourselves; we have forgotten the deep pleasure of spilling our life for another. (2. Eldredge)

Warriors get wounded, and some get killed. Every man's journey in life will eventually face him with the consequences of the mistakes he made in the vigor of his youth. It brings us to our knees and, if we are to move on in our lives, we must recognize the mistakes and what we need to do about them. It will not be easy to recover from the wounds. I can assure you that men begin to make critical self-evaluations during the wounded stage of their lives and this leads either to renewal of purpose, re-direction, spiritual awakening or it leads to being locked in desperation. Henry David Thoreau wrote, "Most men lead lives of quiet desperation and go to the grave with the song still in them." (15. Thoreau)

John Eldredge says, "Let people feel the weight of who you are and let them deal with it." Our strengths must show up when we are in the battle. It seems so strange that a man would not work from his strength in this battle, but many of us are afraid of our masculinity. (2. Eldredge) Yes, we need to grasp masculinity; we need to stop being passive; we must accept responsibility. So where do we sacrifice?

I believe that what a man sacrifices is his male-dominant thinking. He doesn't give up being a male any more than by dying Christ gave up being God. The sacrifice is to stop thinking only male and learn to think female. Learn the re-thinking phrases listed above. Give your wife permission to call out your failures. A bully will need a man to help him grip true masculinity. Learn to listen to her view, her hurts. She will teach you; you must be willing to learn.

The men who make it have learned to bring her alongside them as that quiet submissive help-mate God gave to them. "Right," you say, "but my wife is neither submissive nor a helpmate." I encourage men to share discoveries about sacrifice with their wives. I think it will bring out some interesting discussions.

Remember the toilet seat. Most men rarely consider the dynamics of the seat. We need it up; she needs it down. She complains about our leaving it up. Men don't complain about her leaving it down. Why can't she just work it? Why can't we sit down? Would that be sacrificing too much?

5

The Power of a Homemaker's Submission
Biblical submission and the feminist lie

A woman dictates before marriage in order that she may have an appetite for submission afterwards.

Mary Ann Evans 1870

Man is created to lead, woman to nurture. By God's design women are made to nurture—they want to be mothers; it is natural, wonderful and very necessary. They want to raise children; it's in their genes. And they want a man that they can fulfill. The feminism of the last 50 years has really messed with our families, our wives and us. The biblical concept of female submission to a husband has been so badly misinterpreted by women in the world, as well as in the church, that books such as *Men's Fraternity, Wild At Heart, No More Christian Nice Guy* and *Why Men Hate Going to Church* have sprung up, urging men to raise the level of their game.

Paul Coughlin, a radio talk-show host, in his book *No More Christian Nice Guy*, notes that women are looking for men who show personality and power, inner energy and their own will. He also notes that the man who is passive and referred to as a "Nice Guy," believes his pleasant passivity is God ordained, so he simply assumes there's something intrinsically wrong with women. Either women want a "manly man" to sweep them off their feet or they want to run over every man they come in contact with. This really leaves the passive, clueless man out in the cold. He will either never succeed in leading a woman or will be crushed in the onslaught of an estrogenic avalanche. (4. Coughlin)

This chapter will deal with the submission issue and will have some perspectives from how my wife, Pat, teaches younger women in her ministry. It is potentially dangerous to share this information with men because they might still think that the problem is all hers and ignore the obedience they need to display.

Women's Lib Is Satan's Fib

First of all, we need to clear up one common feminist misconception: Even when women win—they lose. There is no woman-dominant society universally accepted by anthropologists that has existed for more than a brief history. In fact, devastation occurs in women-dominated societies, with the resulting disastrous social consequences (read Isaiah 3:1–12). A recent movie, *The Wicker Man*, is a frightening depiction of a female-dominant cult on an island in the North Pacific that raises and worships bees. Nicolas Cage is induced to come to the island by a complex web of intrigue involving what he thinks is a former lover and a lost love child. Upon arrival he frantically finds out he is the prey and in the end is sacrificially burned in a fire for the good of the next harvest. The disposable drone bee anthropology may work for bees, but it isn't God's design for humans.

Secondly, in spite of the fact that feminism may not be a sustainable sociologic phenomenon, the last half century has seen significant sociologic gains for women. A gender- issues expert, Dr. Warren Farrell, recently wrote that, based on median salary numbers from the Bureau of Labor and Statistics, there are now a number of careers in which women earn more than men. Farrell explains, "When women's pay is significantly greater than men's, it can be in male-dominated fields, female-dominated fields or well-integrated fields." Some positions, where women tend to earn more than men, include sales engineers, automotive service technicians and mechanics, financial analysts, human resources assistants and advertising and promotions managers. (16. Farrell)

It turns out that the strengths of the women's nature and the gender difference accounts for these gains. "The average man would rather be sold to by a woman than by a man," Farrell explains. Women also tend to outpace men verbally and they're usually very good with details and following up, he notes, which enhances their performance.

Because so few women work as automotive service technicians and mechanics, those who do are pioneers, Farrell says, "and whenever people break traditional roles, the people who do the role-breaking tend to be highly motivated and good. They make more because they are so good and because people like going to a woman because it's a novelty."

Female financial analysts earn a median pay that is 15% more than men. Women tend to excel whenever a field such as this requires technical skills plus the ability to communicate and pay attention to details, Farrell explains.

Demise of Feminism

Yet, even though women have clearly made strides in the man's world, all is not well with that progress. The modern history of women, according to Maureen Dowd, can be summed up in three sentences:

Women demanded equality.
Girls realized they just want to have fun.
Ladies long to loll about and what they really want is a man.

Dowd notes, "Forty years of striving have tuckered women out." Today's tired woman prefers escapist fare like *Lifetime for Women* movies, as they are known. (12. Dowd) These programs are about life in stress with a woman's focus and seem designed to vicariously allow women to experience the emotional ups and downs they desire. I will occasionally watch one with Pat, but they are not enough about the conquest, competition and victory for which I am wired. Just give me a Steven Segal movie. Just give me a woman to protect.

The design was always for the woman to voluntarily place herself in the role intended by God. How did it all go wrong?

It turns out the aroma of male power has been an aphrodisiac for women, according to Dowd. It resulted in a several-decades-long rise of feminism, one of the most significant sociologic aberrations of the last 500 years. Well, it also turns out that the perfume of female power is a turnoff for men. Men hoped women would come to their senses, and this may well be turning. Here are some signs of the change:

1. Women moving up try to marry up.
2. Men moving up marry down. The rising professional women on the up elevator have missed all the eligible bachelors on the down elevator.
3. Over one half of female corporate executives annually earning over $150,000 have no children, while only 10 percent of male executives have none. This phenomenon is worldwide, not just in America. Successful businesswomen don't seem to be having children. Some of these feminine corporate climbers used to joke, "I need a wife to cook, shop and carpool." But now many are rethinking and just want to be the wife.
4. According to research in Britain reported by Dowd, the prospect for marriage for guys increased by 35 percent for each 16-point increase in IQ; for women, there is a 40 percent drop for each 16-point increase.
5. In 1980, 44 percent of Harvard female graduates who married kept their birth names; in 2000 that number had fallen to 17 percent and in 2005 a poll by *The Knot*, a wedding website, showed that only 8 percent kept their birth name.

While it may be true on the grand scale of centuries that the feminist movement was only a nanosecond, its effect on male behavior will last another 40 years. The workplace has become a more "feeling" place; men have adapted the skill sets of feelings so that one can now occasionally observe a male pouting about losing the promotion and even sharing in the coffee room the feelings he has about a nasty divorce.

Not only is the office feminized, but so are the original male bastions of politics and sports. The personal saga of emotional redemption has become as important as the muscular, gladiatorial successes. The politician who cannot bare his soul in front of his colleagues with tears filling his eyes and begging for forgiveness is doomed to be a footnote in history. Brett Favre, the most consistently excellent quarterback in NFL history, cried like a baby when he announced his retirement. Men really have learned a softer, fairer side of life and find it very functional and helpful in the legislature as well as in the workplace with women. It also ought to be helpful in the bedroom.

The failure of feminism is not so surprising. It turns out it wasn't much different from the failures of men. In her book, Dowd indicates the demise of feminism is reflected in the Clinton and Martha Stewart scandals. Hilary Clinton stood boldly by her philandering husband and she ran for President. Martha rose from the ashes of financial cheating as a new daytime talk-show host. What this tells me is that women in power can fall just as easily as men; they are no worse and they are no better. What they simply want is power by any means. They will do, say, or be anything necessary to get what they want. (12. Dowd) How is that different from what a man will do?

Hilary Clinton needed to stay in power and needed to love Bill. Rather than take the feminist route and crucify him, she chose to stay with him. She made an amazing run for the presidency and still ended up being the Secretary of State. For that decision alone we should admire her recognition of where the social structure is heading. Martha Stewart simply needed a new TV show.

What they both needed were manly men, in the biblical model.

What they really needed was what Daphne de Marneffe, a clinical psychologist, writes in her book *Maternal Desires*. She noted that it is in staying home and taking care of children that an identity is forged, not forsaken. (17. De Marneffe) This is a huge change, a rather profound truth being reborn from the rubble of feminism; more and more women are discovering it. It is the truth expressed in Titus:

>*...to be self-controlled and pure, to be busy at home, to be kind and to be subject to their husbands* (Titus 2:5, NIV).

Let's Get It Right

Our social and gender relationships are in a veritable washing machine of tumbling outcomes. There really is evidence that women are abandoning the feminist agenda, particularly that part of it that tended to bash and demean men. They are hunting men for their strength and stamina and leadership and to be the fathers of the children they so long to raise. God didn't create them for the roles they thought they wanted, and they are realizing it.

If the man she finds is to be a godly leader, he is to be a servant leader. His role is to lead his wife, but to do so by taking everything about her into consideration and by using his position to give her the greatest opportunity to succeed. There is a new revelation coming about the battle of the sexes. Dowd and Marneffe explain that it may be moving back to an earlier sociologic model. Actually, the apostle Paul wrote about it in Ephesians.

Biblical Submission

The apostle Paul encourages first-century Christians to come out of darkness and into the light in the Lord:

>*Living...not as unwise but as wise.... Therefore do not be foolish, but understand what the Lord's will is...Submit to one another out of reverence for Christ* (Ephesians 5:15–21, NIV).

In this passage the word for submission means to be *voluntarily arranged under someone for your own benefit*. This concept is analogous to a soldier voluntarily placing himself under a commander for his own good, growth and protection in order to accomplish the mission.

In verse 22, we read that women are asked to submit to their husbands as to the Lord as the church submits to Christ. In verse 25, husbands are asked to love their wives as Christ loved the church and gave Himself up for her.

When my wife, Pat, teaches women the biblical concept of submission, it is one of the most powerful lessons of utilizing the power of the Holy Spirit. There is nothing that will motivate a man to love his wife more than a biblically submissive wife.

But be careful here. I am not saying to wait around praying, "God, please give me a submissive wife." That is pretty selfish. Pray only, "God, teach me how to love her with a submission that shows her how to submit."

The natural woman has a curse to slip into feminism, so a man will have to model submission for her. We give ourselves up for our wives. What does that mean? Well, men start by submitting totally to Christ and demonstrating that they will sacrifice themselves for her. That means giving up male-dominant thinking and taking in an appreciation of feminine thinking, pondering it and learning from it.

Now, we will look at an even greater sacrifice for our wives.

⚜

Arnold came to see me because he had been having an affair. When I met with him, he said it started innocently with a woman he worked with. He was not particularly unhappy with his wife; he just started playing with fire. He was greatly dismayed and wanted to keep his marriage alive.

These situations are far more complex than they look and are never innocent little mistakes. The first thing Arnold had to work on was whether or not he really could give himself up for his wife. Yes, he was gregarious and handsome, and he and his wife did attend church.

What he needed to sacrifice for his wife was his popularity with other women. He obviously needed to confess and beg forgiveness from his wife. When he did, she was not able to forgive him at first. Over a few weeks, I discovered why. He was still seen in public with the other woman. When confronted, Arnold admitted that he wanted to continue being with that other woman because "she was fun to be with," but he had no intentions of rekindling the prior relationship. He even tried to invite his wife to come with him occasionally. I asked him if he had confessed his sin to the woman with whom he had the affair and told her how deeply wrong he was to do that. He had not. He was willing to stop some behaviors, having sex with another woman, but he was not willing to reach deep into his character, recognize his evil lust and confess it to God and to his wife. He wasn't willing to sacrificially give up his lustful nature to benefit his wife.

Since Arnold was not willing to sacrifice his fleshly freedom and devote himself to his wife she could not submit to his leadership. They eventually divorced.

The hardest part about counseling is that many of the men I talk to will never change. They get to where they are by making decisions that they cannot or will not undo. It is pretty hard to talk their way out of something they have lived their way into. In the very end, the word sacrifice means that "I am willing to die for you."

Submission Reflects Sacrifice

I realized that Pat and I were both created in Adam and God took us apart so we could come to reflect his gracious plan of salvation for the world. She was specially designed and selected by God to fulfill me; I was specifically selected by God to sacrifice myself for her. Providing I am sacrificing, she will willingly submit for her own protection.

Maybe the following logic will help:

After all, no one ever hated his own body, but he feeds and cares for it, just as Christ does the church—for we are members of his body. For this reason a man will leave his father and mother and be united to his wife, and the two will become one flesh. This is a profound mystery—but I am talking about Christ and the church (Ephesians 5:29–32, NIV).

The Jamieson Bible Commentary states, "A mystery means a divine truth not to be discovered except by revelation from God. This truth, hidden once but now revealed, means Christ's spiritual union with the church is mystically represented by marriage. (18. Jamieson)

So here's the logic: Christ nourishes and cherishes the church because it is His body.

Since Christ left His Father and united with the church, the apostle Paul's writing can be seen as indicating that in order to demonstrate Christ's relationship to the church, a man will also leave his father and mother and cleave to his wife. This mystery was hidden in Old Testament times but made clear with the coming of the Messiah. The reason we are married is to demonstrate God's sacrificial love to the world. That means God's design is for men to sacrifice. Christian men who know this are looking at how much their brethren are willing to sacrifice.

I am not calling for a sacrifice of the sort that Nicholas Cage made by being burned on a pyre for the benefit of the harvest. I am not indicating that a man become a bearded woman either, or become passive and submissive to an estrogen avalanche. What I mean is that men need to understand what the godly calling is for their wives and to sacrifice their own fleshly desires in order to bring their wives to a position where they will be functioning in their spiritual areas. We must die to ourselves to live for someone else.

I found that Dr. Oswalt's explanations to me opened my mind to a higher calling in the purpose of my marriage. It really isn't about us men; it is about the church. It is about the woman and it is about Christ's substitutionary atonement for the world.

I have explained that it isn't about men, so I want to get back to the comment, "God, please give me a submissive wife." I am going to cover some of the details of how my wife counsels women on the subject of submission. Women seek Pat for counseling because their husbands are not understanding them or sacrificing for them. I realize there may be a lot of other reasons that wives may mention, but it is basically because the man isn't functioning in his godly role. So what does she tell a woman whose problem is her man?

Likewise, teach the older women to be reverent in the way they live, not to be slanderers or addicted to much wine, but to teach what is good. Then they can train the younger women to love their husbands and children, to be self-controlled and pure, to be busy at home, to be kind and to be subject to their husbands, so that no one will malign the word of God (Titus 2:3–5, NIV).

Submission doesn't mean being a doormat; it doesn't mean she doesn't also have to submit to Christ or give up independent thought. More importantly, Pat doesn't advise them to give up efforts to influence or guide their husbands or to give in to every demand of their husbands. Since Christ taught mutual submission, the submitting wife is not of lesser value, intelligence or competence. Being timid or fearful is not part of submission, nor does submission imply inferiority or lack of spirituality.

Developing a Domestic Engineer

We first should understand the biblical origin of what *to be busy at home* means. It doesn't mean doing housework. Look at it like being a domestic engineer. In reading the 31st chapter of Proverbs, the idea is presented of how much a woman who seriously takes her God-given role in the home can accomplish. It is not just being at home; it is her divinely-assigned job.

According to Proverbs 31, the woman is virtuous and powerful and:

- Works wool and flax with eager hands
- Provides meals for her family and servants
- Buys property and plants a vineyard
- Works long hours merchandising and marketing linen garments
- Provides volunteer service to the poor and needy
- Ensures that the family is clothed and clothes herself in fine linens
- Has a husband who is respected among the elders of the land
- Speaks with wisdom and manages the entire household very well
- Experiences her children and husband calling her blessed.

Solomon said this kind of woman is worth far more than rubies.

Let's examine the job to do at home. Remember two words: "Helper" and "Nurturer." That's what she's made for. When God gave Adam a suitable helper, that meant he needed one. There was something deficient about men. We were in distress and God came to our need. The woman was something we will recognize immediately, and we will recognize what it is that she will help us with. Remember, she is a virtuous and capable woman.

I suppose some men may not believe that their wife is virtuous and capable. What the Scripture says is that the man has been given a virtuous and capable woman. It's up to him to develop her. When he meets her needs she will become that virtuous and capable woman.

The woman whom God gave you desires and was created to nurture. 1 Timothy 2:15 indicates that women will be sanctified through childbearing; they are designed to nurture—both children and husbands. They are created with an amazingly powerful capability to nurture, to soothe, to comfort, to train. We have already discussed that women today are rediscovering this about themselves. Men should be giving them the freedom to do that.

We have discussed what the women want, what they are expecting. My wife counsels women in that situation to demonstrate a gentle, quiet spirit in accordance with Scripture.

> *...be submissive to your husbands, so that...they may be won over without any words by the behavior of their wives...Instead, it should be that of your inner self, the unfading beauty of a gentle and quiet spirit, which is of great worth in God's sight* (1 Peter 3:1 & 4, NIV)

What this means is that a woman is exhorted to:

- Have an inner quality of gentleness that affirms the leadership of her husband, even when the two do not agree
- Obey like Sarah, without terror (See Genesis 20:2)
- Acknowledge God as an authority greater than herself

What this means for a husband is that submission by his wife means she gets out of the way so that God can deal with him.

If a man wants a submissive wife, consider these principles that we have discussed:

1. Women are tired of being leaders.
2. The unrequited woman defaults to her sinful nature, the "curse."
3. Lead your wife by taking everything about her into consideration.
4. Be sure you are submissive under God for your own benefit. This will model submission for her. You are transparent, vulnerable and repentant.
5. Just as Christ sacrificed, you must sacrifice.
6. Do whatever you have to do to allow her to be a helper to you.
7. Do whatever you have to do to give her nurturing opportunities.
8. Pray that your wife will get out of God's way in His dealing with you. When He does, make the needed change.

What a Man Needs From a Woman

At the risk of allowing men an excuse, I will explain what Pat tells her clients a man needs from a woman. The risk is that some men will remember this list and lord it over their wives. Some might be tempted to look at her lack of these characteristics; others will recognize them as what men really need and probably will say, "Wow, if she did all that I wouldn't have a problem." Men's fraternity teaches that men need the following from a woman:

Companionship
Admiration
Support
Physical responsiveness (5. Lewis)

Yes, that's right, all we need is someone who talks to us, tells us we are perfect, supports our passiveness and indecisiveness and has sex with us. Wait a minute now, I have already pointed out, that we are only going to experience those things after we die to ourselves and meet our wives' needs. The reward only comes after obedience. Waiting for her to be a companion to me before I become her companion will be fruitless.

Paul Coughlin notes that "Mocking men is good business in America. T-shirts with the slogan, 'Boys Are Stupid, Throw Rocks at Them,' were sold in 3, 500 retail stores." Finally a wave of protest had them taken off the shelves. I know there is a real tension between the sexes. The masculine movement seems to be saying that women need to recognize that men will be men, and we just need to have the space to lead. Coughlin is amazed at "…how insufficiently women understand a man's heart and how poorly some wives treat it." Moreover, he notes, "The failure of wives to account for and handle their husband's normal and healthy sexual desires is a form of infidelity that dishonors their spouse." This theory is that real men are adventurous sex fiends. (4. Coughlin)

On the other hand, what I am espousing is that the *feminist lie* is the antithesis of biblical submission. The *masculine lie* is that men are what they are and women need to accept that. Neither model gives me warm feelings. Somewhere in-between all the posturing, the sniveling and the lies, real men need to step forward and pray, "God, teach me how to love her with a submission that shows her how to submit."

We have to finish with the toilet seat again. The submissive wife would never complain about where the toilet seat is, correct? Taking everything about her into consideration that has been learned about our role in her submission would lead us to conclude that the seat ought always to be clean and left in the down position. Whatever needs to be done to accomplish that is a really good idea. Maybe that act above anything else would demonstrate our submission to our wives and lead them to be submissive. Wow, is that a new idea or what?

6

How Do We Stop Fighting?
Rules for settling an argument

The more arguments you win, the fewer friends you will have.

American Proverb

*Those who control their anger have great understanding; those with a
hasty temper will make mistakes.*

Proverbs 14:29

Once we have the revelation that a meaningful, Godly marriage is all
about our leadership and sacrifice, men will need to discover new ways
to recognize the helping and nurturing roles of their wives and how to
talk with them without getting defensive, feeling guilty, arguing, missing the point or sinking to a lower level of relationship.

Dr. John Gottman, from the University of Washington Relationship
Research Institute, says, "Sixty-nine percent of all problems in relationships are unsolvable. They are about differences in personality or
needs. They never change. When you choose someone, you have inherited the problems you will have for the next 50 years. Unfortunately,
we pick people who are not as perfect as we are, so relationships only

work if you wind up with perpetual problems that you can learn to live with." (19. Gottman) Interestingly, I first saw this quote on the side of the white-chocolate mocha cup I get a few times a week at the local Starbucks. Since I am in the marriage business, as well as a physician who has been trained in research methodology, I was struck with this new information. It certainly matched my clinical experience, so I dug a bit deeper into Dr. Gottman's research.

For 16 years, Dr. Gottman led the most in-depth and innovative research ever conducted on the subjects of marriage and divorce. After studying thousands of married couples, he is able to accurately predict whether a couple will stay together or go their separate ways after watching and listening to them interact for as little as five minutes. His accuracy score averages 91 percent. (19. Gottman) Gottman's carefully-analyzed research revealed several behavioral patterns that are present to some extent in all marriages, but more pronounced in dying ones.

The Killers

Harsh Startup involves a spouse who, when discussing a marital problem, launches into personal accusations and sarcasm against the partner rather than the problem itself.

The Four Horsemen shows that negative behaviors, if practiced continually, can be so lethal to a relationship that Gottman calls them the Four Horsemen of the Apocalypse.

Criticism, an occasional legitimate complaint about one's spouse is normal. But while a complaint addresses a specific action, criticism attacks the individual.

Contempt goes beyond criticism. Contempt includes name-calling, sneering, mockery and hostile humor. It poisons a relationship because it conveys disgust.

Defensiveness rarely causes the attacking spouse to back down or apologize. Instead, the defending party usually reverses the blame, creating a no-win scenario.

Stonewalling happens when an emotionally overwhelmed partner (usually the husband) tunes out and sits passively without saying a word or acknowledging his spouse.

Flooding occurs when one partner is so overwhelmed by the other's negative behavior that the focus becomes guarding against the flood of emotional stress the onslaught causes.

Body Language shows a racing heart, perspiration, adrenaline release and mounting blood pressure; all accompany flooding. Clear thinking and problem-solving are negated and the "fight or flight" response kicks in. A marriage with frequent flooding usually ends in divorce.

❧

Jerri's parents were not always as careful about child car seats with their grandchildren, and Jerri's wife, Alice, never felt comfortable with her mother-in-law. So when she once observed her mother-in-law driving the children for a short distance without protection, she expressed great dismay to Jerri. When she didn't feel supported by Jerri concerning the issue, there was a really nasty scene with the parents-in-law. They both came to see Pat and me.

Alice has an uncanny ability to ask the most penetrating, accusatory questions when in an argument with her husband. She can take him down to his knees in a microsecond. During one counseling session I observed her first hand: "So, Jerri, you aren't listening to me. I can't believe you don't feel more concern for our children. What is wrong with you; why do you have so much trouble agreeing with me? Is it because you have someone else you're seeing? You are in denial about the significance of the dangers to our children."

Jerri, in the midst of this onslaught, gamely replies, "Of course I heard you. You are too worried about the children; they are just fine. Why should I agree with you when I think you are wrong and are making too much out of this? It was for only a short distance." Then he threw in the clincher, which happens because he is so frustrated at her accusations, "No, I am not seeing someone else. But, you know, that isn't a bad idea since I can't seem to do anything right for you. At least someone else might leave me alone. You are entirely too pushy about this issue and need to just chill out."

❦

In that exchange I heard the harsh startup by his wife, the criticism and contempt. Then from Jerri came the defensive response to the flooding in order to guard against the emotional onslaught. After that session we were all exhausted.

Alice would first express her hurt and then rapidly go into the attack in almost every conversation. It didn't matter what the subject. She wanted to be heard and understood. Through several counseling sessions we were able to help Alice and Jerri acknowledge each other's position and come to healthier methods of discussion. But Jerri had to leave his parents; i.e., stop defending their behavior which he knew upset Alice and cleave to her and her alone.

❦

Sandra, another woman who had left what she called a totally uncaring husband, once had a phone call with me. She said to me, "He just kills me when he doesn't respond when I ask him for money. Wouldn't you be hurt? How would you feel if someone ignored you? Do you ignore your wife? What do you do if someone won't respond or respect the hurt and shame you have when you have to ask for money? He's always been that way; all men are that way. You really don't care, do you? You just want us to shut up, right? Have you ever had to ask someone for money?" She was becoming agitated, tears were probably coming into her eyes, her pulse was racing and she was ready to go for the jugular!

❦

In that phone call from Sandra, I heard the *contempt*, I felt the *flooding* and I read the *body language* even though I couldn't see it. I wasn't even at fault; I was the counselor, the mediator, and I was the present target for a very misunderstood woman.

I'd like to say that it all worked out all right, that I thought of the right thing to say, but in Sandra's case, I didn't. A woman who has not heard an acknowledgement from the person she is talking to will accelerate her talking and raise the tempo of tension. It was a phone call, and I meekly tried to interject some understanding words, encourage her, but it was all for naught. Finally I hung up the phone. It was not my finest hour. She was already through with this relationship and the divorce papers were already filed. After that call, I felt like I was the one she was divorcing.

The Marriage Formula

As professional people who spend hours listening and counseling people through conflict, we can appreciate the dysfunction caused by toxic behaviors. Pat and I observe it in almost every relationally-troubled person whom we counsel. The startling thing is that they don't realize it. Sandra wanted me to feel her pain; Alice wants Jerri to feel her pain. But raising the toxicity of the conversation to get someone to feel your pain doesn't work. The offended partner either reflects the blame right back or simply goes limp with passivity and withdraws.

After years of studying couples in his research lab, Dr. Gottman came up with an amazingly simple formula for what makes a marriage work. I might call this the marriage formula:

Keep the negative thoughts and feelings you have about your spouse from overwhelming the positive ones.

Interestingly, Gottman was unable to crack the code for saving bad marriages until he began to analyze what went right in happy marriages. His resulting seven principles not only guide a couple in coping with conflict but strengthen the friendship that is at the heart of any marriage.

Principle 1: Enhance your love maps, that part of your brain where you store the relevant information about your partner's world. Learn and discuss each other's goals, worries and hopes. Celebrate important milestones. Especially stay in tune after children come.

Principle 2: Nurture your fondness and admiration. When familiarity breeds contempt in your marriage, it's time to focus on the character traits and abilities that caused you to be drawn to your mate in the first place. Verbalize your partner's positive aspects and nurture them.

Principle 3: Turn toward each other instead of away. During the monotony of daily life, keep your romance alive by letting your spouse know he or she is valued. Care about what matters to him or her and show it.

Principle 4: Let your partner influence you. Gottman says many a man has been derided by his wife for not including her in important life decisions. Consequently, she feels he neither cares about nor wants her opinion. Studies prove that marriages where a husband willingly accepts the influence of his wife are four times less likely to end in divorce.

Principle 5: Solve your solvable problems. There are two types of marital conflict: perpetual and solvable. Sixty-nine percent are perpetual. The key is to recognize and approach them with a sense of humor. Many conflicts are solvable, however, and Gottman offers five helps: 1) Soften your startup (women especially); 2) Make and receive repair attempts; 3) Soothe yourself and each other; 4) Compromise; and 5) Be tolerant of each other's faults.

Principle 6: Overcome gridlock. Stop trying to solve a seemingly unsolvable problem. Instead, acknowledge it as an ongoing sticky issue that you will likely be able to someday discuss without hurting each other.

Principle 7: Create shared meaning. Marriage provides the opportunity for you and your mate to create an inner life together—one that honors both of your values, beliefs and dreams. Be supportive of each other's needs and find ways to honor the differences between you. (17)

Dr. Gottman's seven principles are some of the best reminders I have ever read about successfully living with your spouse. They are characteristics that he found in his research in the lives of successful marriages. They were not characteristics he had observed in unsuccessful marriages. The question here is whether people in an "unsuccessful" marriage can learn to practice these principles?

I have a few simple tactics I tell men with whom I am counseling that they can refer to in the heat of battle. They might not be as flowery as Dr. Gottman's but, when a man is up to his neck in alligators, these will help remind him that the purpose is to drain the swamp.

Satan Starts the Conflict

First, remember that conflict is generated by Satan to keep us from having to do anything meaningful. Second, I want you to understand that you must first forgive and accept yourself, warts and all. This paves the way to acknowledging that many of the criticisms directed at your mate are partially a cover-up for your own self-doubt, an emotion we all experience.

Here they are: **Tactics for Fighting**

Identify the problem. Make sure you both know what you're discussing.

Complain but don't criticize. Address a specific action of your spouse.

Never defend yourself. Christ didn't—and He could have.

Avoid emotional onslaughts. Don't be guilty of flooding.

Maintain clear thinking and problem solving.

Remember the conversation between Alice and Jerri that ended with Jerri saying: "Of course I heard you. You are too worried about the children; they are just fine. Why should I agree with you when I think you are wrong and are making too much out of this?" Then he throws in the clincher, which happens because he is so frustrated at her accusations, "No, I am not seeing someone else but, you know, that isn't a bad idea since I can't seem to do anything right for you. At least someone else might leave me alone. You are entirely too pushy about this issue and need to just chill out."

Let's dissect that conversation:

Identify the problem. Make sure both know what you're discussing. The issue was regarding whether the children should spend time with their grandparents who occasionally didn't use child car seats. It has nothing to do with whether Jerri is honoring his parents by having the children spend time with them or even the remote risk of an accident and injury to the child. It has to do with the fact that Alice, who is the nurturer, and Jerri, the sacrificing leader, are appropriately protecting their children.

Complain but don't criticize. Address a specific action of your spouse. "You are too worried," carries with it a criticism of her nurturing nature. A complaint might be, "I hear that you are concerned with our children, and I am hurt that you think that I am not." It's okay to complain about what she says for how it makes you feel, but it is not okay to criticize.

Never defend yourself. Christ didn't—and He could have. "I think you are wrong..." is a very defensive statement. Jerri is defending his wrong thinking.

Avoid emotional onslaughts. Don't be guilty of flooding. "But, you know, that isn't a bad idea since I can't seem to do anything right for you." That is clearly a flood. In a football game it would be a 15-yard penalty for unsportsmanlike conduct.

Maintain clear thinking and problem solving. "Chill out" is not clear thinking or problem solving. The last thing a woman can do when she is emotionally on fire is chill out.

Steps to Solid Ground in Conflict

We have explored how it should not be. Let's look at how it ought to go. Here's another set of guidelines: When in a conversation regarding difficult issues, clear expressions are very important. Begin the conversation by:

1. Telling her, when she says or does___(fill in the blank)_____. "Here's how I feel…" Now describe what you feel, using emotional words.

2. Next, explain, "Here's what I think…" Enter your opinion here. Remember, this is your opinion, so keep it factual and use "I" words, not "you" words.

3. "Here's what I will own." This is the part of the problem that is mine…. Be ready to confess or modify this by what she says in return. Notice that initially you are clarifying how you are feeling and thinking, and you own your own personal issues related to this discussion. It is not yet time to discuss hers.

4. "I am responsible for my opinions and feelings about this. It is not your fault." You cannot change another person; she is not responsible for how you are feeling about what she said.

5. "I give you permission to help me understand where I might be wrong. I will work on my wrong thinking." This opens the door to her desire to nurture and be a helpmate. But you will have to accept her input and, when you are wrong, admit it and make a change.

6. "Here's what I want." This begins the negotiation.

7. Always say back and forth what you heard the other person say so there is no confusion.

8. Negotiation is best when it comes to a win/win solution.

Now we go back to Alice and Jerri's conversation with these guidelines in mind:

1. *Telling her.* When Alice says, "I can't believe you don't feel more concern for our children…." Jerri could express, "I feel disconnected from you, like I'm defending my parents, or like a worthless husband."

2. *Here's what I think.* Jerri is already thinking that Alice wants to put restrictions on his parents' association with the children. Jerri, on the other hand, is still stuck with them being his parents and having trouble disagreeing with them. So Jerri could say, "I was also worried when they took them for a drive, but I was not as worried as you were. I think it is because my threshold for worry is lower than yours."

3. *Here's what I will own.* "I am responsible for my discomfort with telling my parents about this issue. I am responsible for not being as concerned about it as you are." OK, so Jerri has owned his part of the problem. But he also must be ready to confess or modify this by what Alice says in return. If she makes an issue that she is feeling unsupported, unrecognized or not listened to about the children, he might have to modify his thinking. Jerri would have to do something when she says in return, "You have just said to me that you are more afraid of confronting your parents than you are of not supporting me in my pain."

4. *I am responsible for my opinions and feelings about this.* Jerri could say, "My opinions and beliefs are my own. It is not your fault that I am uncomfortable about this and in disagreement with you. I want to be able for both of us to modify our opinions in order to come to a solution"

5. *I give you permission to help me understand where I might be wrong.* Then Jerri would need to say something like, "I want you to explain to me how my thinking might be wrong. I will work on my wrong thinking." If Jerri is convicted in his spirit that he is wrong, he will want to admit it and ask Alice for

forgiveness. If he doesn't believe he is wrong, that is where negotiation starts.

6. *Here's what I want.* "I don't want to have to tell my parents that they can't babysit with the children. I know that is one solution, but I can't live with that. I want us to figure out a way we can present our sincere concerns about the children without flat-out telling them they can't be alone with them." This begins the negotiation.

7. *Always say back and forth what you heard the other person say.* So there is no confusion, Jerri would say, "I hear that you are very concerned about their cavalier attitude about the children, and you are having trouble trusting them. Is that what you are saying?" Or, "I hear that you are very upset about the way I appear to be not concerned about the children. Which is it, Alice?"

8. *Negotiation is best when it comes to a win/win solution.* At this juncture, Jerri and Alice would now focus on "the problem" that is identified. Both should understand what is troubling both of them. Then both can come to a shared understanding and an approach to their parents that works to diminish the stress in both of them. There will be a few different ways you could solve this one, and each will be correct if you come together as a couple and conclude which path to follow. In this case Pat and I met with Alice, Jerri and their parents for the discussion.

Someone has to stop the fighting and start the healing. Since this book is written for men, I will frame solutions in terms of actions for men to take. Arguing and fighting between couples is part of being together. I feel more alive and alert during a good argument. Strong disagreements and struggles are at the root of the most toxic fights. A recent study from Massachusetts General Hospital sheds some light on the occurrence of fighting in a relationship. "Men who say their wives deliberately pick fights may be on to something," says psychologist Shiri Cohen in *The Week Magazine*. (20. Cohen) Men feel best when they see their wives as happy. Women, in Dr. Cohen's study, on the other hand, are most content when their partners are upset or agitated. "Women tend to want to engage around conflict," notes Dr. Cohen, indicating that this is because a woman feels most connected to her spouse when she can tell her partner is distressed or when the men understand that the women are suffering. Finally, Cohen emphasizes, "the more men and women try to be empathetic to their partner's feelings, the happier they are."

Real men understand that they are the leaders, and there are three inviolable rules of disagreeable discussions to be kept in mind. These rules are like the white lines on the highway that identify the edges. They are like the solid yellow lines that tell us to stay in our own lane. Don't argue with the guy who painted the lines or test the accuracy of where he put them. To do so would possibly kill us.

Maintain the vision of marriage and family. The best marriages are where there is mutual recognition, where a husband willingly accepts the influence of his wife and where problem solving is part of the vision he has for this marriage.

Provide the protection she needs. Often this is a protection from her more easily-deceived character. This is tough because some men believe their wives are, in fact, deceived all the time and they take on the role of correcting them continually. The biblical concept of deceived means only that her nature to help and nurture may occasionally lead to being deceived, and it is the husband's responsibility to protect her from being deceived before she is, not hammering her into submission.

Show her honor and respect. This will move the relationship to the higher level. We have a responsibility to help her develop skills and a ministry. A man is to love and develop her as he would his own body. *He who loves his wife, loves himself* (Ephesians 5:28, NKJV).

Your wife comes into the kitchen while you are eating breakfast. You can tell by her silence that she has issues. "The toilet seat is broken again," she whines.

"What's wrong with it?" you ask.

"I think it is alive."

"Whaddya mean?"

"It's crying."

You don't see where this might be going, but you continue the game. "Did you hurt it?"

"No, I don't think so; I just sat on it like I always do. That's when I felt the tears. Did you hurt it?" She is clearly enjoying this.

"I don't think so; it seemed fine when I finished." Now I get the point. "Do you want me to fix it or just let the toilet deal with it?" I hoped she'd just drop it.

"I don't think it's fair to just leave it alone, I think you should fix it."

"What do you think I should do to fix it?" you ask, pensively.

"Stop using it!" she says—and pours herself a cup of coffee.

7

Two Back Breakers:
Children and finances

Don't throw away your friendship with your teenager over behavior that has no great moral significance. There will be plenty of real issues that require you to stand like a rock.

Dr. James Dobson

After learning ways of working differences to negotiated settlements, this chapter will explore two of the biggest issues which couples have to negotiate that can really scramble a marriage. I do not believe that disturbed children and financial stress are causes of marriage failure, but failing marriages have disturbed children and financial stress. Even satisfactorily functioning marriages have dysfunctional children and financial stress. Marital relational bliss is no protector of the effects of children and money. While this book is not primarily about raising children, since there are plenty of those out there, it is focused on men understanding that they are responsible for leading the success of their marriage. Again, I want to emphasize that the most important thing men can do to lead their children is to model them a successful marriage as God designed it.

Obviously, I can't say that everything went well with my children, as I wrote in the first chapter. It got worse from there. After completing drug rehabilitation, Brett suffered a head injury from a motorcycle crash at age 17 and was in a coma for six weeks. That began another tough chapter as we tried to rehabilitate him again. This was neither pleasant nor successful. Having lost about 40 IQ points, he could remember what he used to be able to do but was unable to do it. His old rebelliousness came back and he was unable to function without supervision, which, of course, he did not want. He died of a medical misadventure involving use of psychotropic drugs being used to control his behavior. I mention that extremely sad incident because raising children, even with the best of intentions, sometimes doesn't come out as we want.

Our three sons are out of the house now; one is in heaven, I am sure, and the other two are raising children. We have reared three children, have read child-rearing books. My wife and I have taught children-rearing courses. I have a medical degree and my wife is a marriage and family therapist. Rearing children is absolutely the toughest job I have ever had to do. Those sweet little things don't come with an instruction manual like my new computer does. Moreover, they are not intuitive, logical or even reasonable. Since we are now enjoying watching our children raise their children, we can observe from a distance. I've noticed something more than I did when I lived with my own children: My experience with grandchildren leads me to believe that the problem with the children is not the children; it's the parents. The children are only mimicking what they observe.

❧

My wife, Pat, was driving around with our two-year-old grandson, Asher, running some errands at various locations. We are very appreciative of child protection seats and air bags that are required by law, but we raised our children with just a seat belt in the back or front so our experience was fairly simple to unbuckle our children and get them out. After several stops, and hefting 35 pounds of grandson in and out of his child seat, both Asher and Pat were getting a bit weary of the buckling and unbuckling.

One of the phrases Pat used with our children when she was trying to get them to comply was, "If you don't do what I am asking you, I'm going to cloud up and rain all over you!" Pat tells me her mother used to say that to her. I suppose her grandmother used to say that to Pat's mother as well. Such is the way traditions get passed.

On arriving at the next stop, Pat asked Asher to help push his way out of the seat after unbuckling him. Asher was tired of this get out, get in, get out drill and probably just wanted either to go home or stay seated, so he just sat there. Pat plopped her hands on her hips, looked into his eyes and said, "Asher, Yia Yia wants you to get out; if you don't get out, I'm going to cloud up and rain all over you!" With a quizzical look, Asher stared at her for a moment, then quickly came to some conclusion that included the possibility that if he didn't comply, his grandmother would somehow rain all over him. I am not sure what sort of picture that produced in his mind, but it got the intended result. He got out of the car.

Later, at home, he was being encouraged after supper to get ready for bed and his mother told him that Yia Yia would give him a bath. Pat was on the phone to a friend and Asher said, "Take a bath, Yia Yia?" Pat said, "Just a minute, Asher; Yia Yia is on the phone." Well, he stopped in his trudge up the stairs, looked at Pat with a glare and said, "I'm going to rain all over you, Yia Yia!"

❧ ❧ ❧

What I will say about raising children in this chapter won't be a long dissertation but rather a short synthesis of what I discovered that worked really well, a few things that didn't work well at all and a lot of things that I've read or heard that I wish I could have tried.

Raising Moral Kids

Gary Ezzo, in his book *Raising Kids God's Way*, notes that in rearing children, parents commit three mistakes:

1. *They manipulate the children by creating the fear of losing Mom or Dad's love.* This leads to a *conditional love* becoming the motivator for right behavior. Please don't break a child's heart by saying, "Daddy doesn't like you when you do that." Listen to this: "When you do that, Daddy doesn't like the way you act, because I know you are a better boy than that and I love you."
2. *They manipulate the conscience by making the child feel guilty.* This leads the child to *avoid guilt* as the motivator for right behavior. "Johnnie, only evil, bad boys throw snowballs at girls." Johnnie wasn't thinking he was a bad boy, but now he's heard that the seemingly harmless act of throwing snowballs makes him evil. That's a lot more damning than, "Hey, Johnnie, I know how much fun it is to throw snow balls. Here, let's throw some at each other for fun. But you know, little girls don't like having snowballs thrown at them and I know you don't want to hurt them.
3. *The parents fail to provide the moral reasons for behavior.* Constant fear of punishment, reproof and rejection becomes the motivator of right behavior, not the true love of virtue. (21. Ezzo)

The goal in child rearing is the production of moral virtue as the reason for behavior. When focused on the moral-virtue thinking, we can say to the child who is shyly not saying hello to a guest in the home, "Lanie, in our home we show respect to guests and say hello and shake hands. This is because we respect them and want to show them we like them and appreciate that they have come over to our house."

You don't say, "Mommy won't love you if you don't say hello to Mrs. Johnson," or "Lanie, what a terrible little girl you are. You are very naughty and you know better than this; now go say hello to Mrs. Johnson."

Then, the parent may have to take the child by the hand, or pick the child up and assist the child in making contact and then praising her.

Manipulators—How Cruel

So why do parents default to manipulation? I thought that the little devils were so illogical and unreasonable that it took a brilliant parent to get ahead of them. Actually, it does take a brilliant parent to get ahead of them, but it turns out that there are better ways than the manipulation of guilt or conditional love to achieve moral growth. I think parents manipulate because they don't know what to do and lack confidence in parenting skills. That's what I did. I just wanted to be a friend, or dictatorial, or controlling and not a mentor. Children don't need parents to be friends; they need teachers, role models and mentors. Their friends are their age. I advise parents who still have trouble with the parent vs. friend concept to go to their local community college and take a parenting class. Don't keep making the same mistakes.

The following are a few key verses that have always kept me focused on how I was to teach my children rather than to manipulate them by strong negative feelings.

By wisdom a house is built, and through understanding it is established (Prov. 24:3, NIV).

Love the LORD your God with all your heart and with all your soul and with all your strength…Impress them [these commandments]on your children. Talk about them when you sit at home and when you walk along the road, when you lie down and when you get up (Deut. 6:5 & 7, NIV).

The rod of correction imparts wisdom, but a child left to himself disgraces his mother (Prov. 29:15, NIV).

No discipline seems pleasant at the time, but painful. Later on, however, it produces a harvest of righteousness and peace for those who have been trained by it (Heb. 12:11, NIV).

I have no greater joy than to hear that my children are walking in the truth (3 John 4, NIV).

The Basics

Here are six teaching moments from lots of conversations with parents and from family instances in my own home. They don't cover all the situations, but I think they'll hit the highlights. They really are the teaching moments I made an effort to default to in my thinking:

1. Both parents should agree on basic principles of moral absolutes, what kinds of behaviors are unacceptable, and then strive to teach the child "why." We need to spend time coming together to decide on these principles and rules. Rules should apply to us as well. If tardiness is one of the rules, it applies to us, too.

Pat is a wonderful cook. She made it a priority to always have an evening meal with our family, and the way it was served to all of us family-style was the envy of the neighborhood. As our children grew older, there was often a challenge to get everyone to the table at the same time. She was hurt when we had to sit and wait for everyone to assemble, some from playing outside, some from the television and me from doing work in my office. I wanted to establish with our children that coming when asked showed their mother respect and admiration for the wonderful meal we were about to enjoy. Everyone could enjoy a hot meal; a prayer would open the mealtime and we would all enjoy the fellowship. We all discussed how important it was and concluded, with everyone's eventual agreement, that if anyone was three minutes late after Pat put the food on the table, that person didn't get supper. Pat used an egg timer to monitor everyone's compliance.

It took a few days for our three sons to get the message and there were some hungry bedtimes. Then one evening, I guess I overestimated the egg timer and arrived at the table from my office to the cold and heartless stares of my sons and a wide grin on Pat's face. I gamely stated, "Sorry, everyone, I just had to finish that project. Pat, this looks great, let's pray." My oldest son, Mike, said, "Dad you're late; the timer is over." Everyone immediately chimed in, "You don't get to eat." Pat quickly added, "But you could pray for the rest of us to enjoy the supper." I did, they did enjoy it, and I went back to my office. Later on Pat fixed me a sandwich after the boys were in bed. She told me that's what she did for them when they missed supper.

2. Chastisement should be followed by a loving explanation of why it was necessary. It should be used only for acts of rebellion, active or passive, and ceases at about 11–12 years of age.

My father was the chastiser in my family. He chose to use a 24 inch x 1 inch piece of a picket fence as the whip, which my siblings called it. When our rebellion particularly frustrated our mother, we would usually be advised that we were going to get a whipping when our father got home. I remember where he kept the stick. It was over the dining room door. I still have vivid pictures of him reaching over the door frame as he called out one of us to have the pleasure of being the example for the rest of us. It was usually two swats for the boys and one for my sister. I didn't understand the reasoning for that, and she didn't get very many, as I remember, but I guess it seemed gentle. None of we boys thought he whipped her as hard anyway.

Dad asked us to put our head between his legs and while he held us in position, he applied the full measure of discipline we deserved. Then he always asked if we understood why he had spanked us, extracting a confession and lovingly telling us that this would help us to grow in obedience. The sting of the swats usually wore off in a few minutes.

So I took this example into my own family. I spoke about Brett's rebellious, stubborn streak earlier and he was the one most likely to be required to put his head between my legs. What I didn't grasp was the need for me to do this discipline lovingly, after prayerful reflection. I remember being angry at how rebellious he was, being at my wits' end and thinking I could put some sense into him. He had very skillfully lied to his teachers and to his mother and me. Lying, in my book, was a rather serious rebellion. I remember it was more than two swats and it wasn't with a piece of picket fence. I think it was my college fraternity pledge paddle, a rather sturdy piece of hardwood. He was almost 13 years old and was too tall to bend over and put his head between my legs. My first clue that this wasn't going to work was that I told him to lean over his bed and, while swatting him, I noticed him gritting his teeth without a single tear or whimper. I stopped and tried to begin the loving teaching, but my anger was still inside of me and he knew it. He wasn't going to respond in deference; he wasn't remorseful and simply didn't say a word. The next morning, as he was walking into the shower, I noticed that there was a small bruise on his rear end.

Brett and I did work through this experience and he became a rock-climbing and skiing buddy. I never spanked any of my sons after that day, and now I think the limit is one or two swats with a small wooden spoon. I think we probably ought to have another way to discipline children after they are ten years old. Thirteen is way too old; the rebelliousness that occurs at that age is a serious matter and at that age children are capable of reason, other consequences, and are far more able to resist us than an eight-year-old.

3. Child-centered parenting produces self-righteous children. The need to understand God's order and respect in their world leads God to the center of their universe, and not themselves.

Alex and Ruth determined that their children were the focus of their lives. They believed that their children should be free to make choices from a very young age, and they would not interfere with their choices, unless they were dangerous. Therefore they pretty much allowed their children to behave in any way they saw fit, tried not to be too stern and found themselves explaining to friends and neighbors why their children were terrorizing the neighborhood. Their oldest seemed to confiscate all the other kids' toys and would throw a tantrum when rebuffed. Bedtime was whenever the child went to sleep, wherever each might be at that time. Food was always available, and Alex and Ruth were proud that their children were so independent. We didn't care to have our children play with them because we had a different way of discipline. We could tell that the demands made on the parents were trying, but they stood firm about not being firm. These children grew up, but they became very narcissistic and manipulative, ultra-liberal in their approach to life, and to this day can't be persuaded to think more highly of others than themselves.

It has always seemed strange to me that a person who advocates, "Every man ought to do as he wants," will someday wonder why there is so much chaos in the society around him.

4. Vary the response to their behavior and keep them guessing. I learned to vary the response but not to vary whether I responded. Right is always right and wrong is always wrong; we should respond to it every time. Children can, and will, outlast us and are masters at pushing the limits.

It is a challenge to be consistent with children. They are supposed to grow up; they are supposed to find their limits and ours. They will make mistakes and will test us; they will want us to define the limits, both because they want to know we care and because they want to know where the safe zone is. I preferred to keep them between the fences, but they just wanted to move the fences. So Pat and I had to keep changing the fences.

Most mothers really get upset by children's messy rooms. Our son Erik, apparently, was not born with the hang-it-up gene. Nor did he get the put-it-away rule when I was instructing him. Pat said my mother wished her good luck when we were engaged because, "I could never get John to clean up after himself," so I think I didn't get the hang-it-up gene either. I realized how important it was to my helpmate, so I tried a number of various responses to the mess in Erik's room. Of course I didn't see his mess because I didn't get the gene either.

First we tried what my mother and father had tried, keep a daily chart above the bedroom door of how clean the bedroom was and reward improvement in Erik's effort. That didn't work for Erik. Pat reminded me, after two weeks of trying the chart, that my mother once showed her the one she completed for me. It was still above the door in my childhood bedroom. It had no improvement trends either.

Then we tried picking up after Erik and hiding the stuff somewhere else. That didn't work. He would come screaming into the kitchen moments before the school bus arrived, naked from the waist up, "Where did you put my shirt? Do you want me to go to school naked?"

I had the brilliant idea that we would pick it up and make him pay for the clothes to get them back, the logic being that I was paying his mother to keep the house clean and if she had to pick up after him, he should pay for housekeeping services. That didn't work. He didn't have a job and I didn't believe in child welfare.

Then Pat got the absolutely brilliant idea that she was going to pick it up and take it in a basket to school, walk into his classroom and dump it on the floor around his desk. She cleared it with the teacher and Erik was dumbfounded when she ceremonially dumped the stuff, saying, "I want you to feel comfortable in school, so since you seem to like a messy room, I thought I'd mess up your space here." That did work.

The next week, I returned to my office at the hospital to find my dirty clothes on the floor around my desk. My secretary said Pat had been there and commented, "Since John messes up my home, I thought it only fair to mess up his office." That worked, too.

5. It is not appropriate for only one to always be the disciplinarian. Parenting is not a good guy/bad guy arrangement. However, God's order establishes the husband as responsible to raise his children in the love of the Lord and that means the buck stops with the father.

Because my father was always the disciplinarian, I had a great deal of respect for him, but he was unapproachable as I was growing up. I suppose my mother felt protected, but Dad was distant. We trusted Mom more and could always talk to her. When we were in trouble, the words, "Wait until your father gets home," struck fear into our hearts. I felt like I needed an appointment to even talk with him. As a result I grew up to think of God as heavy-handed, more like my father than my mother.

I wanted balance in my family, and Pat and I had to agree on the rules for our children. When I was not at home, she was the disciplinarian; she didn't have to wait for me to get home.

It was the babysitters we had to worry about.

Pat and I were gone for a weekend and left a young couple, Ray and Rebecca, with our children. The boys knew the rules, but the sitters didn't. One morning Rebecca looked out the kitchen window to the swimming pool and noticed that Mike had moved the trampoline from its location 10 yards away from the pool up to the edge of the pool and was jumping into the pool from the trampoline. As she went screaming out the door to stop him, she glanced over to the fireplace chimney and nearly fainted. Brett had attached my climbing rope to the roof and was rappelling down the chimney. No harm was done, and everything was put back in its place. The rest of the day, the boys had quiet time in the house under Ray's watchful eye. Ray had to be the good cop. After all, he and Rebecca had no children yet. But discipline was by the bad cop, Dad, when we got home. I actually thought it was somewhat humorous, but I needed to point out to my sons that Ray and Rebecca were pretty overwhelmed with their tricks and we expected them to glorify God with sedate activities when parents weren't around.

6. When a child is punished beyond the crime, or has a consequence which is out of his/her grasp, or sees a double standard of behavior, that child will be provoked to anger (See Ephesians 6:4).

I had always wondered what actions provoked a child to anger. Just because I said there was no more bedtime story and the lights were going out, there was an occasional frantic outburst that looked a lot like anger. But it probably wasn't because, if it was, I had to tell another story and I was bored with reading and the child needed to go to bed. I don't think stopping the bedtime stories when I wanted to was provoking in a biblical sense.

Had I taken the prerogative when I was late for dinner to simply sit down and eat, acting as if the rules of tardiness didn't apply to me, I would be provoking the children to anger. When my son missed a curfew by 20 minutes, to punish him with, "You're grounded until further notice," would be a bit extreme. He would have nothing to shoot for, his punishment would be without end, and I would have provoked him to anger. Brett was our pianist and there were times when he had to be rather sternly disciplined to practice. I wanted him to succeed at the piano for his own self-worth. He didn't take well to academics, like his brother Mike, and I believed he could make up for that by being better at the piano than his brother. Well, he was very good, but whenever I put a consequence of practice time beyond his attention span or while his brothers were playing in the yard, he was provoked to anger.

Once I told him, "Brett that sounded really great, but if you play it again and improve the part of the runs, I'll put a gold star on the page for you." He thought about it for a moment and then said, with a grin on his face, "Dad, if you'll tape a dollar bill on the page, I will play it very, very well. Gold stars suck." I learned a lot that day, so I let him go play with his brother. I didn't know that gold stars were a provoking element.

Teenage Years

Adolescence is a period of rapid change. From the children's ages of 12–17, children's parents age an average of 20 years. When children get into the teenage years, something drastic happens. They learn to talk and argue. They are only trying to establish their independence, relate to what all their friends are doing and see how far they can move parents off their sense of right and wrong. A Christian counselor who spoke at a teenager seminar I attended tells it this way, "For every 10 minutes the argument with a teenager lasts, the parent loses 10 years of your age. Pretty soon it is two teenagers fighting it out."

That same counselor showed me a helpful diagram (Figure 1) of the parent's roles and responsibilities with teenagers. Before a decision is made with a child, remember first that your job is to love the child and to state the rules and consequences. If the child has been told something a thousand times and still hasn't gotten it, who's the slow learner? (22. Presented at a counseling conference in Denver)

PARENTS' JOB: Love the child.

It is not our job to make the decision about what the child is going to do. After the child makes the decision, our job is to enforce the consequences, support the child and congratulate him on his decisions.

TEENAGERS' JOB: Leave home.

The teenager, on the other hand has a responsibility to leave home, listen, ask questions and understand the situation and the consequences.

It is their job to make the decision. After the teens make the decision, it is their job to accept the consequences, feel good about the outcomes and take the credit for their decisions.

	Pre-Decision	Decision	Post-Decision
Parents' Job:	Present rules	None	Enforce Consequences
	Monitor situation		Support
LOVE	Help child understand		Congratulate
	Clarify consequences		
	Observes the child		
Teens' Job:	Listen	Make	Face consequences
	Ask questions	Decision	Feel good about outcomes
LEAVE	Understand consequences		Take credit for successes
HOME	Understand situation		

Figure 1: Roles and Responsibilities in Teenage Decision-Making

Dr. Richard Berry, in his book *Angry Kids*, writes about five behaviors parents engage in that teenagers are particularly upset by. Dr. Berry calls these five toxic behaviors:

1. Bringing up the past.
2. Attacking the person rather than the misbehavior.
3. Making compliment sandwiches.
4. Intimating the teen must be good to earn our love.
5. Offering no opportunities to regain trust. (23. Berry)

I pretty much understand the value of avoiding the first four of those teenage toxic behaviors, but I find the biggest problems in understanding how to help a teenager regain trust that they have lost from really bad choices. Parents have an innate belief that is expressed to their child as, "Show me you can be trusted and I will give you an opportunity to do what you want." Whenever we say, "No," to a request from teenagers and indicate that it is because we think it is dangerous, too tempting or wrong, we aren't allowing them to grow or discover for themselves where the limits are. With this sort of approach the children are learning that they have to demonstrate that they believe or behave like us before they can express their own independence. In rebellion they will say, "Give me an opportunity and I will show you I can be trusted."

This sounds like a Mexican stand-off. If we never give them opportunity, they are really thinking, "Because I can't trust that I will ever get another opportunity, I'm going to take full advantage of the situation while I am doing what I want."

❧ ❧ ❧

Our oldest son, Mike, was a good student and a basketball player in high school. He was almost never in trouble and I could trust him with just about any circumstance to make right choices, or so

I thought. After turning 16, he expected a car and I bought him a van. He liked it because it had a boom box set of speakers in the back end. Unfortunately, the car was not mechanically sound, Mike was not mechanically interested and the car was becoming more trouble to maintain or repeatedly get fixed so it would start reliably every morning. So we traded it in on a small Ford Escort. I instructed him that he would have to check and change the oil and maintain the car. He had a job at the local movie theater and was more than able to manage the task of maintaining the car.

After several months with the car, I heard him go out to the car and try to start it one morning. The sound coming from that car's engine was a mechanical screech of metal rubbing on metal that brought me to attention in a hurry.

"That doesn't sound good," I said to myself as I ran to the door. Mike kept trying to start it in spite of the screech and the lack of a successful start. The screech of metal on metal of an engine without oil is a sound that is worse than the screech of fingers on a chalkboard. I heard the sound and was running outside telling him to stop just as the engine froze up.

He had a quizzical look at me and stated profoundly, "Something is wrong with the car, Dad."

"No kidding. Have you checked the oil?"

"Yeah, I think it was OK," he said, but with a lack of conviction as to the veracity of his statement.

"When did you check it?"

"Uh, I don't remember, but it's been a while, I think."

"Well check it now." I said.

After showing him how to check the oil, we discovered that there was none. Now I had an issue of trust with Mike. Although I don't remember for sure, I think I told him that I was not going to ever buy him a car again until he could be trusted to take care of it. Of course I was frustrated, angry, overwhelmed at his lack of mechanical interest, and I think I was even a bit remorseful for not being more specific about how to check the oil.

These kinds of situations with teenagers are problems for every parent. In this situation, I wish I had the model I just discussed about whose job is whose.

My job is to love and instruct the child and to enforce consequences. His job is to understand consequences and to take responsibility and credit for success. But there was no success. The engine was ruined and the car wasn't worth enough to justify putting a new engine in it. But I still had to love the child and instruct the child. How many cars would I need to give a child before I could quit instructing or helping him? Does God have a limit on trusting us?

I have five siblings. As teenagers, all of us completely wrecked a car that was either given to us by our father or was one of his business or personal cars. That is six cars my father lost to teenagers. None of us ever felt his wrath for those losses. Immediately after rolling over a funeral-home limousine in a snowstorm when I was 16, with my mother in the passenger seat, he trusted me enough to make me get back in another car and drive it home.

I helped Mike get another car; the consequence he had was to have to make a small car payment and he did learn about responsibility with cars. He is the safest driver in our family and I don't believe he has ever had a speeding ticket, an accident or failed to care for a car again.

What he did do with that next car was to get a little careless with the monthly payments and fall enough behind that the lender repossessed the car from his driveway. He called me one morning saying, "Someone stole my car, Dad."

I knew he needed to learn the value of money management.

It's The Money, Stupid.

When we are counseling couples, we always spend a session or two on the economic engine running the family. We rarely find a couple in crises that are not also in crisis with their finances. I don't think the finances are the cause of the problem, but a broken marriage is usually broken in most aspects, such as communication, fair fighting, finances, children and sex. We need to work with them to smooth these out.

I have been responsible for managing multi-million-dollar budgets in my business career. I have created limited liability corporations, obtained a Master's in business administration and have been a chief administrative partner of a medical practice. I have prepared budgets and financial reports for my partners. The consequence of a misstep in the finances of a business can mean lower shareholder profits, failure to achieve business goals, bankruptcy and dissolution of a partnership. The same inattention to financial affairs in a marriage can lead to divorce, loss of children and social failure. In spite of our experience and the advice that we share, most of the time when we get to the point with a couple that we need to heal their financial situation, they stop coming. I suspect this is because they know how difficult it is and would be embarrassed at how little planning they have done. Almost everyone without a financial plan is in trouble.

Budget, Budget, Budget

If we do get a chance to advise clients about financial planning, I start with a budget. Budgeting means getting a solid idea of the priorities that the family has about spending money. Both husband and wife should agree on what is on that list. Next, determine how much is coming in and how much is being spent by listing income and recurring expenses. Average them out to a monthly average from the data for the year. The total of required spending is the minimum income requirement. We will discuss later what to do if the spending is more than the income because we first have to discuss tithing and saving.

Tithing, Tithing, Tithing

Tithing is giving from the first fruits. Saving is paying us. If we are doing neither, we have a serious faith problem. The purpose of this chapter is not to explain how to make a budget or how much to tithe or to save; if it isn't done by a family, some professional advice on how to do it may be a good idea.

Harmful Debt and Debt Reduction

Debt is a problem with almost every person whom I counsel. They expose their wife and family to financial pressure, constant calls from creditors, anxiety about whom to pay next, worry about what might happen if they aren't able to earn an adequate income and uncertainty about future financial independence. The young millennial generation is among the worst offenders of very poor money management. Many don't balance checkbooks or track bank balances, depending rather on very expensive overdraft protection. They may use paycheck cashers that charge one to four percent instead of their own bank and take out high interest payday loans. Ken Rees, CEO of *Think Finance*, writing in *USA Today*, characterizes millennials as financially illiterate, under-utilizing savings, accumulating debt and having no access to credit. He uses a term called "under-banked" to characterize their failure to plan financially. They tend to use alternative financial services that come with a higher price tag but make money immediately available. (24. Rees) They will wake up some morning and find that their income doesn't equal the spending. Banks, credit card companies, car dealers and even mortgage companies will offer access to more money than we can ever repay because they can garner high rates of interest and penalty fees. They really do make a lot of money from people's money mismanagement. Every week I get an offer of a new credit card, a second mortgage on my house or a note saying, "You have been preapproved for a $20,000 loan." It is very easy to outspend our income by debt spending.

Men who are in the situation of spending money beyond their means have an addiction and should seek professional financial help.

ͽoͼ

In our fourth year of marriage I had had enough of spending one evening a month paying the bills, so I had a discussion with Pat and asked her if she would take that burden from me. I was an intern at the time, and the tradition at Johns Hopkins Hospital was that the intern lived in the hospital and was always on call. I argued that I simply didn't have time to pay the bills and still try to get a few hours of sleep. So she agreed. That began a several-year period in which we continually had difficult discussions about money, mostly because we didn't have enough. So we sat down and developed a budget. Pat had always wanted a budget, but I wasn't quick on the development of one.

She came to me one day with a handful of envelopes and said, "This is the way my mother always ran our house, so let's try putting your paycheck in these envelopes in cash and when there isn't any money in one, we'll just have to not pay that or take it from one we do have some money in." Sounded like a reasonable thing to me. I said, "We have to be sure we have enough money in the ski-trips envelope." That was when I first saw this look on her face that I later learned meant, "You don't really understand that the problems we have are because you spend too much money." I was still operating from the position that she was the one who spent too much money; after all, she was writing the checks. However, we did agree to talk about how much went into each envelope and to have a civil discussion about which envelope we would take money from to meet the bills. This exercise was a life-changing experience.

Eventually I began to notice that Pat was experiencing the same frustration that I experienced earlier when I asked her to do the bills. It wasn't just that there was time involved in paying the bills. That was the easy part. The tough part was when there were more bills than money. Pat would tell me that there were more ski trips than money. I also remembered that my mother never managed the household money when I grew up and that I didn't remember my parents ever fighting about money. That had not translated into my marriage.

Our church sponsored a financial counseling seminar by Larry Burkett and that opened my eyes. I learned, of course, the usual principles of budgeting, tithing, planning and saving, but what really struck me was when he told us that three financial pitfalls will break a family: 1) Harmful indebtedness; 2) An unrealistic lifestyle; and 3) Unrealistic expectations coming into marriage. That seemed reasonable, but then he told us, "A husband must take the lead in the establishment of a budget and avoiding harmful indebtedness. The woman's major need is security. It is the man's responsibility to provide for her security to the extent he is able-bodied and trained. If his "work" does not provide, then he has two choices: 1) Change his vocation to earn more money; or 2) Scale back their lifestyle.

Well, I decided that I was failing in my responsibility and the first thing I did was to take back all the bill paying and assume responsibility for the unrealistic lifestyle and harmful indebtedness we had gotten into. Each of us needed to understand our spending habits and agree together to a debt-reduction plan. Many men believe the solution is to put their wives to work. I chose not to do that because we both wanted Pat to raise our children.

When I found myself responsible to make our budget and lifestyle work, we started to get along a lot better. I did take on some moonlighting jobs, changed cars, kept my skis a couple years longer, joined a ski patrol so I could ski for free and made a few other successful changes.

❧

Sara Allen is executive director of the local Consumer Credit Counseling Service in Fort Collins, Colorado. In a piece she wrote for the *Denver Post*, February 2005, she said,

"Living under one roof and sharing the money that comes into the household can be a daunting task. Getting a handle on the money decisions that need to be made in the household can go a long way toward keeping the peace in the marriage. There is no right or wrong answer. Just do not put joint money decisions on autopilot. Couples should agree to a system for giving each person some autonomy about what to spend the family money on. On payday, maybe they should each keep some cash for spending, even if all they can afford is $20 each. Or maybe set a limit on the amount of money that can be spent without consulting the other. This would keep a new car from showing up in the driveway.

"It is also not unusual for one partner to earn more than another. Have a discussion about how to handle that. Pay the bills and divide up what's left, or split expenses 50/50. Or does it make sense to prorate expenses so that the partner earning more pays a higher share of the common expenses? The only wrong decision when it comes to how you will spend your money is to not have the discussion.

"Who will handle the monthly bill-paying obligations so the bills get paid on time? Ideally, each partner should take a turn at this so that both have a handle on where the money is going. But if one person is better at this, by all means choose the partner who is going to be good at following through. Remember, both are affected by the credit report, so it's important to have a system for timely bill paying." (25. Allen)

Dual Income Family

Here are some ideas I have found for living with the 21st century concept of dual-income families. I know that most families have more than one income and, in some families, the major breadwinner is not the husband. Neither of those situations is in opposition to God's Word. When I get involved with couples whose relationship is in crisis, one of the areas we have to deal with in counseling is the issue of dual incomes.

Let me reemphasize again about the God-intended nature of helping and nurturing for a wife. My comments now are made in the context of a husband's being a breadwinner. I will explain some basic rules of engagement for working wives. Her primary work is in the home. When there are children at home, this is where she ought to be. I know that some homes have dual incomes they depend on. I also know of homes and families where the man is the primary caregiver at home while the wife with the larger income works outside the home. But bear with me to the end and then make a decision about how to handle this issue.

Sociologists have studied the phenomenon of day-care children. There is evidence that this is creating children who are overly aggressive, lack intimate emotional development and are not family-unit oriented. Additionally, it places overly-tired parents with an over-stimulated child in the evening.

The husband is to understand and develop the spiritual gifts of the wife that may allow her to work in the home when the children are at home. Her work is to be a ministry, involving nurturing and helping others. When the duties in the home lessen, she needs to spread her area of influence throughout the community, to the church first, then the world. When there are no children yet, or the children are gone from the home, or the children are old enough to fend for themselves at home, or she can work from home, a working wife is just fine. There are many successful and godly women who work long hours and still have effective godly homes. My own two sons have had to deal with these issues. One has chosen to have himself and his wife work full time and they arrange schedules so he can be with their daughter rather than use day care after school. My other son and his wife both quit their jobs in a resort community and moved to a city where he could make sufficient income to allow his wife to remain at home while they raise their children.

In two-income families, the husband is still responsible for the budget setting even though he is not the primary breadwinner. There is a considerable risk to the family if the "second income" is used to meet routine monthly expenses. This dependence on the second income places too much pressure on the wife to avoid her homemaker responsibilities in favor of bringing home the paycheck. It calls for planning by the couple for family time, savings, discipline and cooperation. It places the stability of the economic engine of the home at the risk of unexpected pregnancies or ill children. I know that the stability of the economics can be interrupted by an illness or death of the husband as well—but that is what insurance is for. The likelihood of childhood illness or unexpected pregnancy is not something that can be insured against, and both are more common than the death or disability of a husband.

When working women are surveyed, 60 percent preferred a marriage where they did not have to work outside the home. The economics of dual workers indicate that the average increase over a similar family with one working husband is only about 25 percent more income. Dual workers means expenses for child care. The 100 percent more time invested by the wife in work is returning a relatively low economic dividend.

Finally, with a working wife and children who would profit from the nurture of a mother at home, here's how I think God can bless the situation since she is already working:

The second income should be used for: 1) Education savings; 2) Home down-payment but not mortgage payment; 3) Vacation fund; 4) Retirement planning; 5) Completion of the home with pay-as-you-go.

Adopting this approach would force some extensive planning for the good of the children, the retirement years together and the beautification of the home.

A Word about Design

I know that the foregoing thoughts are not really popular in the present generation. Some recent books demonstrate the broad spectrum of opinion about this issue. In her book *To Hell with All That*, Caitlin Flanagan writes that women who are averse to the traditional domestic role detract from the quality of men's and children's lives. Flanagan's major points: 1) that most women hate housework but want to be good at it anyway, 2) that women say they want men to contribute an equal share in the domestic arena but don't want to sleep with the kind of men who do, and 3) that married people should have sex, are hardly revolutionary.

What makes Flanagan's book original and vital is that she is a realist willing to acknowledge, for example, that when a woman works something is lost. That is not an indictment of a working mom, since

Flanagan makes allowance for those who try to make it work. However, she makes it clear that any sensible working mother can see the truth in such a statement— time spent working equals less time with children equals something lost. What's appalling is that pointing this out raises such ire among those who would rather not consider the consequence of their choice to work. (26. Flanagan)

On the other hand, Linda Hirshman's book, *Get to Work*, presents the case for the women filled with ire who would consider domestic duties as an anathema, something never to be sought in any way. Her book is a notoriously blunt analysis of child rearing as a waste of well-educated women's time and talents and greatly minimizes any proposition that the process of caring for and about children can contribute to women's self-actualization. Such is the difference between these two views. (27. Hirshman)

I do believe women can be bank executives, firefighters or police officers and not only mothers, nurses or teachers. What I said earlier was that a woman's work is to be a ministry involving nurturing and helping and that, when the children no longer need her nurture or help, she should be able to work doing whatever she wants and her husband encourages her to do throughout the community, the church, then the world. Almost any work involves nurturing and helping. So I am not against wage parity or equal opportunity and am not gender-biased toward any profession.

I do have to admit that I simply don't understand why any woman would want to be a professional football player. While I might agree that every woman should have the equal opportunity to play professional football, there is still my conviction that the first woman place kicker on an NFL team will be an interesting person to meet. There might be some deep-seated desire to prove herself in a man's world. I just can't imagine why on earth one would want to. But then, I am not a woman, although I know my wife would not want to play football. She hates anything that makes her sweat. I just believe God's plan is for the woman to be the primary nurturer in the home—a role she fulfills better than any NFL placekicker can.

There are really differences between men and women besides anatomy. They are positional and functional differences, not brains, not wisdom, not verbal skills. God's design for responsibilities and positions in the relationship does determine what we should do. This is a God-designed not a man-forced position.

The Bible teaches role differentiation for men and women. Husbands are the heads, the top, or source, of their wives (See Ephesians 5:23), and men are to be leaders of the family as well as the church. Having a man leading the family and the church is essential for Christian harmony and success. It applies in the marriage relationship regardless of how a man and a woman may think. The principles and doctrine of family and church leadership cannot be made to be feminist without either dropping some large chunks of the Bible or explaining them in a new exegesis that is ultimately unsound.

While Jesus introduced great liberation into human life by His accepting attitude toward women, other than divorce, His words are silent on the relation of women and men in marriage as well as on the polity or authority structure of the early church. His comments on divorce were the result of questions from men and were directed at men who were the divorcers of the day. Women didn't have that option. As we have seen, women have enjoyed greater freedom and true gender equality in recent decades in the Western world. I must again reiterate that my comments about leaders, sacrifice and submission, whether we are discussing marital fidelity, management of children or finances, can be seen as running counter to equalization of the sexes. Nevertheless, they are timeless and true principles that do not depend on our agreement with them to make them correct. That is what God's will is for.

We are in an age where the rise of feminism, must be addressed by the evangelical church. In past times, the traditional church has been guilty of suppressing women both in the family and in the church. That should no longer be our desire or motivation. There is great beauty in the relationship of women and men in the church. The delicate interplay, the give and take between man and woman (a mirror of the redemptive relationship between Christ and the church) speaks nothing of superiority and inferiority but only of a vastly fulfilling love that welcomes the differentiations God has assigned. The perfected union of a man and his wife is a model of mutual submission within the operation of the church.

One final thought on children from my experience. Pat would regularly complain to me that I needed to teach the children how to use the toilet seat. All three boys suffered from the idea that the toilet lid was invisible and didn't really move, so they used it wherever they found it. I wish I could give advice about that problem, but I can't. I tried to train them, with little success. My mother used to say boys are harder to yard-break than toilet train. After all, our plumbing was designed to require a minimum of effort. For my sons, it didn't matter where the lid was if their aim was bad.

8

Clearing the Conscience
Help, I'm hurting

The torture of a bad conscience is the hell of a living soul.

John Calvin

Up to now we've dealt with concepts, rules and experiences and not so much with masculine thinking. In long years and hours spent delving into lives of men in crisis, I have come to learn that what they really need most is to change the way they think. And at this place in the book, I am not talking about how to think feminine; I am talking about how men can change the thinking that results in their failure as men. When we fail to understand our wives in marriage, there are character defects which account for some of our failures. This is the thinking that needs to change.

In Chapter Four I spoke about thinking patterns that may cause men to not understand or perform their role in the marriage. Here they are again, without the nicknames:

Insecurity about masculinity
Desire to control all situations

Attachment to the physical
Unrealistic personal expectations
Ignorance
A seared, guilty conscience
People pleaser

Thinking a Man Has All the Answers

In this chapter we'll explore changing this wrong thinking. I will explain a logic that will help us to recognize when thoughts are likely to be wrong. This exploration is designed to bring a man to the place where he can realize what thoughts and attitudes need to be taken captive and changed. Finally, how to make the change will be discussed.

The book of James notes:

What is causing the quarrels and fights among you? Isn't the whole army of evil desires at war within you? You want what you don't have, so you scheme and kill to get it. You are jealous for what others have, and you can't possess it, so you fight and quarrel to take it away from them. And yet the reason you don't have what you want is that you don't ask God for it. And even when you do ask, you don't get it because your whole motive is wrong—you want only what will give you pleasure (James 4:1–3, NLT).

James is saying that we do all kinds of evil things to get what we want, including fighting. But God doesn't give it to us, even when we ask, because we are selfish. Basically, we want what we want when we want it. We'll fight to get what we want. Selfishness and personal pleasure are the reasons we want it. So the logic from the epistle of James is, "Your thoughts are wrong when you are in conflict." This brings us to a discussion of conscience.

The Conscience

The conscience is the scene of the desires at war within us. Conscience means *with knowledge, with awareness.* It is the portion of our higher intellectual functions that learns the consequence of right and wrong in moral issues. Our conscience starts out when we are infants, not knowing differences. It is innocent and pure, sort of like a computer hard drive with no program written on it. All of our life experiences add to the hard drive and either commend us for correct moral decisions or condemn us for wrong moral decisions and actions. The judgment of the rightness or wrongness of the decision is a combination of spiritual, sociological, psychological and intellectual experiences. Most of our learning as children comes from the adverse consequences of behavior. The conscience is not only built from all the good and happy things that happen to us, but the bad and unhappy things as well.

I think we all understand that two-year-olds do not innately become unselfish, always lovable cherubs who do not manipulate people and situations for their own good. Hardwired into all of us is a strong sense of self-preservation and self-pleasing. Our response to stressors in our environment is either fighting to overcome it or fleeing from the threat.

A two-year-old may suddenly rip the toy out of another child's hand yelling, "Mine," at the top of his lungs. The child has not thought through how unkind and uncaring that move is. Some subsequent event is going to have to teach that child's conscience the moral correctness or incorrectness of the action. The other child may stand up, pick up another toy and throw it directly into the face of the first child. That's a pretty solid indication that the behavior is risky. The child's parent may step in and use words or actions that will modify the child's understanding of the value of swiping toys.

After a certain number of experiences, most children's conscience moves them to avoiding upsetting another child, and, one way or another, they develop a reasonable conscience. Eighty-five percent of our moral judgment has been developed by the time we are six years old. At that age we have learned ways in which we will respond to relationships, stress or threats throughout the rest of our lives. For example, we can learn from observing our parents that physical abuse is one way to control the activity of a wife. We can learn that murder is wrong from experience, observation or someone teaching it to us. It is also possible that we can watch enough TV and pornography that we conclude that a sexual relation with someone not our own wife is OK, as long as we don't get caught. The moral judgment is filed away into our memories as a conscience, burned onto our hard drive. Fortunately it is not a *Write Once Read Many* (WORM) drive because it can be rewritten. That's where God comes in.

The Bible teaches that men can so harden their hearts that their conscience is seared. That was the state of affairs with the Pharisees in Mark 3:1-6, when Christ showed them the man with the withered hand and asked them if it was right to heal someone on the Sabbath, i.e., was it legal to do good deeds on the Sabbath or is it a day for doing harm. They did not answer Him and their silence angered him. Mark 3:5 indicates that He was angered because their hearts were hardened, that they had no conscience. The minds of the Pharisees had been blunted by their own sense of legalistic self-righteousness.

This blunting of the conscience is important to understand. The conscience is designed to either commend us for good or condemn us for bad. That's how a healthy conscience works, and that's a good thing because we must always be trying to increase the commending and decrease the condemning. But that is not the case with a seared conscience, a blunted conscience or a hardened heart. That situation applies to a man who is clearly doing wrong and has absolutely no inner voice or feeling or spiritual tugging or anything that convicts him that he is wrong. The Pharisees were simply not aware that they were so wrong. That is what angered Christ.

The principles filed away in our conscience direct our daily decisions about what we do, what we accept and how we process new information; our conscience will control our attitudes and actions.

So what happens when we experience a broken relationship and are suffering? Some principle of our conscience has taken us down the road to trouble. Remember, suffering is necessary to accomplish God's best and pain is designed to be a test to let us know our own deep life principles. The test brings the junk in our lives to a level of consciousness so we can remove it. We can remove only what we know is there. If our conscience is telling us to change something, just do it. If we are experiencing relational pain and aren't getting a clue from our conscience, we have a seared conscience. That calls for a different level of personal effort to just do it.

Without a clue from our conscience, we start to think that pain comes into our life because of what someone else is doing. A seared conscience will make us think it is far easier to blame someone else than to take a good hard look at our own issues. It is one thing to think as the world thinks and blame it all on our wives and quite another to decide that our own disordered belief is at the base of the failure.

Transforming the Mind

Don't copy the behavior and customs of this world, but let God transform you into a new person by changing the way you think. Then you will know what God wants you to do, and you will know how good and pleasing and perfect his will really is (Rom. 12: 2, NLT).

Our transformation is an activity that occurs in the mind and it means that we stop looking at something as we see it and let God change us to see it the way He does.

In the fifth chapter of Matthew, we read how Christ taught His disciples the way to clear their consciences in a discourse of Scripture known as the Beatitudes. He exhorted and promised them a blessing when He said, *God blesses those who mourn, for they will be comforted* (Matt. 5:4, NLT)

To mourn is to have a godly sorrow about our impure hearts, our unclean hands and our double-mindedness. This mourning is a sorrow of immense proportion and it rises from the depths of a man's soul. It drives him to do something; he cannot stop until he finishes. The same word is used in other places in Scripture: It is like mourning the loss of a loved one, or as the merchants of the world *weep and mourn* because of the destruction of Babylon that we read about in Revelation 18:11.

Mourning involves the conscience, that portion of a man's mind that either commends or condemns him. When condemned, we need to take action. When in pain, but our conscience is quiet, recognize that the apostle Paul describes this situation and he strived *always to keep my conscience clear before God and man* (Acts 24:16 NIV 1984) We find it painful to live without a clear conscience.

Clearing the Conscience

"The willingness to truly forgive each other is also important to a successful marriage," says Dr. Daniel W. Zink of St. Louis' Covenant Seminary. "But Christians have to be careful in this area. We know the Bible says to forgive, so we rush into it without dealing with the root cause of a problem. I believe to really forgive we must face the hurt straight up and deal with it openly and honestly. Then we can let it go and move on." (28. Zink)

Dr. Zink points out that simply forgiving ourselves or someone else is not all of the process. This process is essential to the Christian faith. Facing the hurt and dealing with it means we have taken that fearless and searching personal inventory, discovered what folly our thinking is and become willing to get beyond it. Dealing with the root problem means repetition of the issue is dead.

The first action is what the Bible calls *repentance*. This word in Greek is *meta noeo* and it literally means to change our minds. It means we are making the correct response to our conscience as it condemns our thinking. No longer do we call what we do right but, after repentance, we call it wrong. That's all it takes to begin. If the Pharisees could have simply said, "Christ is right; this all-rest-and-no-work on the Sabbath is pretty demanding, legalistic stuff" and said, "Where's the good?" they would have gone a long way toward clearing their consciences.

Next we are called to *confession*. The Greek word is *homo lego*, which literally means to call our action what God calls it—sin. We agree with God that we are wrong. Here we are to confess to God as well as to one another. Many of the people we know are aware of our character defects anyway. They may be one of our best allies in renewing our minds.

This leads to *forgiveness*. The word in Greek is *apo hiemo*, which is an accounting term, meaning to clear the record. Forgiveness means we have received assurance and believe the issue is sent away, balanced by the sacrifice of Christ, and is no longer of any importance. Credits and debits are equal and the books are balanced. God's forgiveness is unconditional and already given for everything we have ever done.

There is, of course, the matter of root causes and consequences of our thinking and behavior that Dr. Zink spoke of above. We must make *restitution*. The Greek word is *apo kathestemi*, meaning reversal of consequences. Order must be restored. There are no consequences to God; there are no changes that God must do; it is up to us.

Forgiveness is a two-way street. Not only must I ask for forgiveness, but so must I forgive others. Sometimes we must be the ones asking for it and sometimes we are the ones giving it.

<u>Forgiveness is:</u>
Giving the person a clear record.
Yielding my right to defense.
Giving the offender over to God for correction.
Being willing to suffer the pain of offense.
Acknowledging the nature of God.
Being conformed to His image.

<u>Forgiveness is not:</u>
Just forgetting.
Easy, because we just want to get even.
Cheap, the price has been paid.
Transferring the hurt; we will still suffer.
Doing the person a favor; it's doing us a favor. After all, now the other person will be dealt with directly by God.

Pat's day started very early. The trash collectors outside our town-home bedroom window were dumping the large dumpster into the trash truck. The adrenaline rushed into her body as the sound ricocheted off the walls of our room. As she awoke she glanced at the clock, hoping it was 7 a.m. The numbers had a different story, it was 5 a.m. The last time she saw the clock it was 1 a.m. as she tried to fitfully get to sleep earlier. "Four hours of sleep," she grumbled. "How will I even function today?" She glanced over at me to see if I was awake. I had merely twitched briefly and was already snoring again. "Why doesn't he wake up?" she wondered. "Not much sense going back to sleep because I know I won't." She got up and went into her study to pray, read and just be angry that the workmen woke her up.

Her Bible study class was that morning and she always liked to be rested before the time of fellowship. "Why does God do this to me? Doesn't He know I need to be rested to teach the class?" She noticed a slight sore throat and muttered, "Great, now I'm getting a cold, too."

I woke up to my alarm at 7 a.m. and noticed Pat was not in bed. Walking down to her study, I heard her typing on her computer. When I asked her why she was up so early, I got this vicious comment about the quality of the men the condo association was contracting with to clear our trash. "They must be pretty stupid, because they don't even know what time it is." It certainly didn't help at all when I said, "Well I didn't hear them." The flesh on her face was tired and beginning to crawl into her eyes, so I quickly perceived this as a high-threat environment and muttered, "I'll go shave and shower."

It got worse from there. That evening she was going to leave on a five-hour drive to Salt Lake City for a weekend women's conference. I was working until noon at the hospital. When I got home, Pat was frazzled because she had spent an extra hour after the Bible study with one of the ladies in need of some counsel. She had just closed her eyes for a short nap when I slammed the door coming in and hollered, "Hi Babe." She responded with a slight growl and I saw her suitcase packed by the door.

The vicissitudes of a worn-out woman are a sight to behold, and great caution is required of any man who dares to walk into it. I calmly walked up to her and asked, "What's going on?" Honestly, I had for-gotten about her Bible study and her drive to Salt Lake City. For a microsecond the thought crossed my mind as I looked at her suitcase that she was moving out.

Then I experienced 10 minutes of emotional expression from a fire-breathing, estrogen-charged woman who felt tired, unappreciated, unprotected and absolutely inconsolable. She could have even consid-ered taking her suitcase and moving out. She asked me if I remembered where she was going. I didn't. She wondered if I thought she might be tired. I had considered that possibility and gamely even asked if her friend might be persuaded to drive most of the trip. That didn't set well because, "That wouldn't be fair to her." She went on, "Why don't you call the trash people and complain about their coming so early? I can't believe my own husband and best friend doesn't even know what I am doing. It's almost like you don't even care."

Her friend arrived and a brief truce was called. I went upstairs to do something and I don't even remember what it was. She called out, "Aren't you going to carry down my suitcase?" I came down and took it out. She did stop long enough to give me one of those functional kisses that women give just in case something terrible happens. They'd at least know they kissed a husband goodbye.

I said, "Honey, I was so wrong to be insensitive and forgetting your trip. I don't have any excuse for that and you are correct that it doesn't reflect well on how I pay attention to you. Will you forgive me? I want you to have a fun time and be blessed with the conference."

She said a cold "Thanks" and left.

I walked upstairs and within two minutes, my cell phone rang. "John," she said, "I was wrong to blame you for the way I was feeling unappreciated. Will you forgive me?" Instantly, our relationship was reestablished—really, in an instant. My heavy heart, knowing that we weren't going to see each other for four days, suddenly lifted. I knew everything was going to be all right, and so did Pat. We were both com-forted as God had lifted us up. But I need to tell you that we have had to work really hard to not let the anger go to sleep with us anymore.

Here are steps for clearing the conscience.

1. Confess our failure to God and receive His forgiveness.
2. Give the person complete forgiveness.
3. Do not tell her of this forgiveness unless she asks for it.
4. Confess to the person whom I have wronged what biblical principal I violated and that I now am admitting was wrong.
5. Ask for forgiveness.
6. Make the life change that reestablishes the relationship, makes restitution and restores order. (29. Oswalt)

In the Twelve Steps of recovery used by Alcoholics Anonymous, the process described above is covered in these steps .

1. Make a searching and fearless moral inventory of ourselves.
2. Admit to God, to ourselves and to another human being the exact nature of our wrongs.
3. Be entirely ready to have God remove all these defects of character.
4. Humbly ask God to remove our shortcomings.
5. Made a list of all persons I have harmed and become willing to make amends to each one.
6. Made direct amends to such people.
7. Continue to take personal inventory and when I am wrong promptly admit it. (30. W)

Applying the Steps

Insecurity about masculinity usually comes from a disordered youth and either conflict with father or absent father or from observing a disordered father. This kind of masculine injury requires the following thought process:

First, come to grips with defining what it is that identifies masculine misfits. Am I fearful? Do I hate conflict; does intimacy frighten me? Sometimes hearing from a brother in Christ what he thinks the issue is can be helpful. Maybe the issue comes from always needing to be in control. Maybe it is aloofness and always being alone.

Then repent. Confess to God the new change of mind about the behavior that has been wrong. Call it what God calls it. "God, I am so-o-o wrong to hate conflict so bad that I don't come to the support or protection of my wife when her boss mistreats her. I hate being such a wimp. I have failed to provide protection for my wife." Then receive forgiveness from God. Stop a moment and reflect. God promises that when we confess our sins, He forgives us and cleanses us from all unrighteousness. He has already forgiven.

See how God has presented himself. He is a loving father who disciplines those He loves and will not stop working in their lives until He has perfected them. If being a wimp is a result of an abusive father, recognize that it is not correct to assume that our Heavenly Father is also abusive. He is not. Visualize the strength of Christ.

Now I give my father complete forgiveness. Maybe it was my mother who abused me or who wasn't there to befriend me. I can't blame her. God only expects me to forgive those who fail me, abuse me or are my enemy; He doesn't expect me to hate them, blame them or forget them. I must forgive them.

Next it's time to go to those who have been affected by my behavior. It could be parents; it might be my wife. It will probably be my children. Confess to her/them my sin and specifically say, "I was wrong." Don't just say, "I'm sorry." The latter doesn't mean anything— only that we are upset that we got caught.

Ask specifically for forgiveness. Don't just confess and wait in silence for the other person to offer to forgive. Ask for it—"Will you please forgive me?"

Making the changes to demonstrate that God has touched our lives completes the process. It is the restitution, the correction, and it will restore order to a disordered life.

The desire to control all situations comes from being a control freak. Our masculinity is tied up with being in control—lording it over another person. Control freaks usually have a co-dependent relationship from their own childhood where obvious dysfunctional behavior was very upsetting. That person has learned to control situations in order to feel normal. This character flaw requires something like the following thought process to change:

First, realize that it is God who is in control. None of us can add a day to our lives by our own personal effort, so it is best to simply accept God as the master and search for what He is calling us to do.

We need to forgive all the people who hurt us or failed us in our youth. More than likely most fathers really do love their sons, but some fathers didn't show it in the way we would have liked. Mothers can be absent as well, working full time or depressed, possibly struggling with abuse of prescription drugs, and they just weren't there for us when we wanted them. The hardest person for any man to forgive will be the priest, the man next door, the scout leader or the boy down the street who sexually abused him. Yet we must forgive him. That is what mourning means.

Now we who have been wronged will have to go to our parents, brothers and sisters, spouse or children and come clean about trying to control events in their lives and creating unattainable expectations that we held up to all of them and to ourselves. We demanded performance, behavior and perfection. We had to plan everything to the last detail because we couldn't stand the unknown or having to repeat something. As control freaks, our sense of well-being was tied up in controlling them. We were trying to modify or change someone else's behavior to make us feel better. Go to them with a godly sorrow about the behavior. Confess it to them; ask them for forgiveness.

Now we make the change. God is the master of the universe and He has a plan for us and everyone else. We are not responsible for someone else's plan, only our own. Make the change.

Attachment to the physical sounds like many guys. Looking at Playboy magazine or Hustler, masturbation, demanding lots of sex from their wives are unhealthy behaviors and some of us even get into drug addiction, gambling or other addictions. Maybe it is marathon running or Play Station games. Addictions usually begin in a subtle manner and end up hooking us because we have a brain propensity to addictions. Drugs, alcohol, cigarettes have specific drugs that can be used in treatment to counteract the cravings for addictive substances, but pornography and behavioral addictions are not treatable by drugs. Men who struggle with this problem need individual counsel and a strong man who will hold them accountable to the changes they need to make.

Addictions are very difficult and require a spiritual realization that we are powerless over the effects of them in our lives. It might be a good idea to throw away the Play Station or computer that is taking our time, or put it in storage. Replace it with quality time with our wives and families.

Once free of the addiction, we use the same steps of confession and requesting forgiveness and making the change that we have already talked about. This sets things straight with those we have harmed by our behavior. Once again that process is what it means to mourn. We are so convinced of our error that our hearts are broken and we cannot live without expressing that great sorrow to those whom we have harmed. Addictions eventually kill us. They don't just give us pleasure; they kill us. Addicts die a death of mental or physical failure from drugs and alcohol addiction. Lungs will eventually stop working from smoking. Pornography will eventually replace the sense of satisfaction from healthy sexual relationships, and this will kill the marriage. The picture is not pretty.

Unrealistic personal expectations can cause many men to labor under the idea that they are better than they really are. That isn't the problem. The problem is when we persist in behaviors hoping to produce the end we want when those behaviors have repeatedly not done that.

I worked with a physician once who believed he was destined to be the next Nobel Prize winner based on research he was doing with AIDS. There wasn't a single other physician who knew him, or his research, who thought there was any chance. Yes, he had a large lab and was doing some pretty cutting-edge stuff with vaccines, but we all knew that the solution to AIDS was not going to be a vaccination. He was obsessed by it; he was losing his credibility over it. Actually, Thomas Edison labored from a similar problem, but eventually he found out which combination of wires, glass and vacuum would produce a light bulb. In effect, as he said, "I have not failed. I've just found 10,000 ways that won't work." Edison didn't give up and we have General Electric because he persisted. In the instance of my physician acquaintance, fortunately he decided that the pursuit of this dream was futile. Today, 23 years later, there is still not an AIDS vaccine and he is volunteering his services in an underserved area free clinic to add to his practice of medicine. That will probably get him more credibility for his future than his attempts at discovering an AIDS vaccine.

I realize that there is a fine line between greatness in performance and a life of mediocrity. The motivation to pursue a personal expectation, goal or dream is not the issue here. We all need to realize that our goals must be achievable and make sure that they will not interfere with the relationship we have with our wives. In the movie *The Astronaut Farmer*, actor Billie Bob Thornton and his wife and children were the only ones who believed the former astronaut could actually build a rocket and attain near-earth orbit. He was obsessed by it and it consumed his life. However, it did not destroy his family who helped with the project. It is a moving story as he is successful in spite of the efforts of the US military and NASA to prevent him from launching.

How should we deal with the issue of personal expectations? In the next chapter I will discuss letting go of personal expectations, which Dr. Oswalt indicates are really setting us up as little gods. It is a process that begins with recognizing that our self-righteousness is dysfunctional and therefore we must give up our authority by sacrificing our self to the higher good of service to our wife and mankind. My AIDS research physician acquaintance probably found that truth later in his life

A man and his wife sold out to any idea can win in spite of very powerful opposition. On the contrary, being sold out to a notion, but ignoring the relationship with our wives, will be costly in spite of very powerful personal expectations.

People pleasers habitually give in to other people because they just can't stand the thought of upsetting them, or they put their own needs to one side because they get a buzz from someone else's happiness. The medical term is codependency. The happiness of codependent people is dependent on other people being pleasant and kind to them. The false belief that they are operating from is, "If I am kind to them, they will be kind to me." The problem is that when they act this way they frequently find that the other person is not a bit grateful. Therein lies the rub. People pleasers come from an environment where they were always elevated above their circumstance by their parents, always told they were better than they actually were, and they learned to seek their approval from people and not to trust anyone but themselves. So how is codependency dealt with?

Kindness does not equate to "people pleasing," nor does unkindness equate to disagreement. It is possible to be both kind and to state our own needs. Standing up for yourself is not being unkind.

People pleasers need to change from wanting to please people to wanting to please God. The only report card they will ever really need is the one God writes. Each man must do what he is called by God to do, not called by his wife or next-door neighbor to do. If we are gifted, and a task is a particular joy to us and we are called to do it, then we should do it. By not doing the task that brings us joy because we are doing something to please our neighbor, we are robbing our neighbor of having the joy of doing something himself. Or, we are robbing the right person whom God will call to do the job. Our job is to do our calling and leave everything else alone. John Eldredge says this, "Let people see the real you, sold out to Christ and devoted to serve Him. If that is offensive, let them deal with it because you can't please them." (2. Eldredge)

Of course our Christian frame of reference requires us to treat all people with politeness, dignity and respect. If they aren't nice to us, that is, if they do not treat us with politeness, dignity and respect, then consider limiting the relationship. Don't respond to rudeness with rudeness; it just perpetuates the problem. We shouldn't keep returning with hat in hand trying to get on their "good side" to help us feel better.

Some of the above advice is not necessarily related to the husband-wife relationship. If a wife is asking her husband to do something for her, wearing himself out doing it may not necessarily be people pleasing. It's just smart for a man to meet her needs for security, significance, comfort, etc., as we have discussed in earlier chapters. Even if fixing a leaky faucet or clearing out all the unsightly weeds she sees out of her kitchen window is not our thing, we probably ought to do it.

Men who are big people pleasers need to set things straight with those whom they have harmed by the behavior. It will be the same steps of confession and requesting forgiveness and making the change that we have already talked about. Once again that process is what it means to mourn. The truth of mourning is in becoming so convinced of our error that our heart is broken and we cannot live without expressing that great sorrow to those whom we have harmed.

Now we must make the change. When we are drawn to people pleasing again, remember that God is the master of the universe and He has a plan for us and everyone else. Start small. Find something small to say "no" to, but say it firmly. Say it politely, but mean it. The world will not collapse around our ears. People rarely take offense, and those who do aren't worth pleasing. We are not responsible for making someone else happy. Others are not responsible for making us happy. The Holy Spirit is the source of true happiness. Make the change.

But suppose she asks, "Where would you like to go to eat tonight?" Men, be very careful thinking about this answer. The way we handle this can either take us into marital bliss or put us into the mental wasteland of an *Abilene Paradox*. (31. Harvey)

The Abilene Paradox

This paradox is a classic business-school study of how people make decisions counter to the real preferences of the people involved. A family living in Coleman, Texas, is comfortably playing dominoes on the front porch on a hot summer Sunday afternoon. It is in the 1960s and the father-in-law suggests that they all go to Abilene for dinner, 53 miles away, in their non-air-conditioned car. His daughter says, "Sounds like a great idea." The son-in-law, despite having reservations about the bad restaurants he knows in Abilene and the long, hot July drive, is feeling like his preferences are out of sync with the rest of the family. So he says, "Sounds good to me. I just hope your mother wants to go." He is surprised to hear her coming to the porch with more cool lemonade saying, "Of course I want to go. I haven't been to Abilene in a long time."

Well, the windows in the car are all down, the hot wind merely moves the heat around in the car and doesn't cool anybody off, and the cafeteria where they eat has really bad food. They arrive back on the porch four hours later exhausted. Not a lot of conversation had occurred.

Back sitting on the porch with the fans running, someone says, "It was a great trip, wasn't it?" Clearly this is not an honest statement. The mother-in law grumbles that she would actually have preferred to stay home, but went along because the others seemed so enthusiastic. The son-in law says, "I knew it would be a disaster, but I went along to satisfy the rest of you." The daughter-in-law says, "I just went along to keep the peace. I would have to be crazy to want to go out in heat like this." The father-in-law then says, "Well I only suggested it because I thought you all might be getting bored."

They all sit back perplexed wondering how this could have happened. None of them wanted to take the trip. All would have been perfectly happy to sit comfortably on the porch but did not admit to it when they had a chance to enjoy the afternoon at home. (31. Harvey)

Now how on earth could that happen? Every one of us has done that sort of thing. We have answered our wife's question about where to eat by giving an answer she wants to hear and she was asking the question because she wanted to please us. Well, that delightful family in Coleman, Texas, was no different. They were all people pleasers, wanting to make others happy, from the father-in-law, who was probably already bored himself, to his wife who thought everyone else was happy with the decision and didn't want to let anyone down. Even the son-in-law, who knew it would be a disaster, went along.

The earlier question, "Where would you like to go eat tonight?" is fraught with danger. To escape the trap, the husband must really evaluate the lead-off question and answer first with personal honesty, then ask for clarification. First, simply answer the question. We tell her where we want to eat and let her deal with the answer. If it is Taco Bell, just say so.

I have discovered that the problem may be that women may be asking the question hoping we will select some place that they really want to eat. They want us to read their minds, picking their favorite restaurant. No problem, we just speak to that possibility with something like, "While I like Taco Bell, I can't read your mind, and you probably do not. Since I really do want us to enjoy the evening together, I think you might like Chez Paris better and that would be okay with me." We have been honest with what we want and we have told her what we think she might like and that it is okay with us. That's as good as we can play this game because we cannot read her mind. If any one of the family in Coleman had said, "I don't want to go to Abilene; I am perfectly happy to sit here with you all. It will be a hot trip, but if all of the rest of you want to, I enjoy your company and I am willing to go," I suspect they would not have gone.

The people pleaser in this restaurant story would pick a restaurant he does not like because he thinks it is the one she likes. That is saying, "No matter how I feel, this is what she wants." She probably already knows which restaurants he doesn't like and will think less of him for saying, "Let's go here," when he really doesn't want to. Better to suggest Chez Paris and wait to see if she bites on it.

Simply let your "Yes" be "Yes," and your "No," "No"; anything beyond this comes from the evil one (Matt. 5:37, NIV).

What Is the Comfort of a Clear Conscience?

We are innocent when our conscience is clear. Paul was compelled to clear his conscience daily so that his message of the gospel would not fall on deaf ears. The people watched Paul's behavior; they would know if he was not living what he was teaching.

Having a clear conscience also quiets those who would speak maliciously against our good behavior. It also means that we are prepared to give an answer to anyone who asks the reason for the hope we have. Okay, the reason we need to clear our conscience is because we cannot enter into a new way of seeing things if our conscience is seared. Therefore when the circumstances in our lives present us with a truth that we are convinced applies to us, we clear the conscience.

I think we start by making a list, beginning with those closest to us. Then list the biblical wrong that the Holy Spirit has brought to our attention.

PERSON	BIBLICAL WRONG
God	Unbelief
Parents	Failure to honor and obey
Mate's Parents	Failure to honor
Spouse	Failure to understand, honor, love, submit, right thinking
Children	Inconsistent, provoking to anger, failure to Discipline
Relatives	Failure to maintain family relationships
Employer	Failure to give a full day's work, or honor or speak well of
Employee	Failure to provide instructions, a fair wage, opportunities to learn
Friends	Failure to be transparent, considerate, thoughtful, encouraging

With our list in hand, we go to the person. Bill Gothard's Institute in Basic Life Principles taught me this principle 20 years ago and I remember even having a little cheat sheet of how to go to someone I had wronged to confess: (32. Gothard)

"I have been looking back at my life and I realize now that I have failed to conduct myself in a godly way in relationship to you. I have ___ (fill in the blank) _____ and I admit this violated God's principle of _____ (fill in the blank) _____and I was wrong. Will you forgive me?"

~o&~

My father was sort of speechless when I sat down to do this with him face to face, but I had already forgiven him. I had learned the Bull of the Woods principle from him, but I didn't blame him for that. If we are still angry at someone, or blaming him for what we have become, we call that the victim mentality. It has actually been used as a defense in some criminal and moral failures that have occurred to people, sometimes successfully. In reality, we are still controlled by the person with whom we bear a grudge rather than being free from the bondage and behavior that resulted from that anger. No, my father should not have taught me some of the things he did, but then I should not have taught my sons some of the things I did and they should not be teaching their sons some of the things that they are teaching. I then confessed my wrong to him and asked for his forgiveness.

Dad said, "Of course I forgive you, son." I knew he meant it and I received it for what it meant. I no longer needed to be bound by him and felt accepted and approved by him. I could go on with my own family.

What I had to apologize for was how I had dishonored him in our community by my rebellious behavior and for disobedience when I didn't follow his rules. My older brother and I used to crawl through a window into his funeral home garage and drive around town in one of the limousines he had. Once we took 13 kids with us to the dollar-a-car night at the drive-in theater. We were too stupid to know that the owner of the theater knew Dad as well as the car. On one occasion we played with matches in the old barn near our house and burned it down.

Another event which I had to mention to him was one of the urban legends of my home town. I was a sophomore in high school and the school year had just started in September. A new family had moved into a beautiful Spanish-architecture home a block from our house. They erected a six-foot-tall white stucco fence around the property which significantly hid the pretty house from view. I overheard people talking about what a shame it was that the community couldn't enjoy seeing the nice home anymore. So my friend Bobby and I began plotting a way to get some payback for erecting the fence. We came up with a plan to sleep outside in bedrolls Friday night and get up in the middle of the night to paint *NUDIST COLONY* in bright red paint on the lovely white fence.

My younger brother, Tom, noticed us out in the garage getting out the red paint and wanted to know what we were doing. We, of course, didn't tell him, but we also wouldn't let him sleep out on the porch with us that night, much to his chagrin.

The event went off very well; we neatly wrote large red letters on four sections of the fence, each about 12 inches tall, noting not only that it was a nudist colony but where the entrance was located. We were back in the bedrolls by daybreak, sound asleep.

I was awakened by my father at about 6:30 a.m. as he asked me to go with him to make a hearse run with him to the local hospital to pick up a man's remains and transport them to his funeral home. We had to drive right by the white fence.

I sat quietly in the front seat of the hearse as we stopped at the stop sign next to the fence. I didn't even look at the sign. My father did. He said only this, "If one of my sons did that, I'd whip him within an inch of his life." I don't remember whether I said anything at all, but I remember nothing else was said. I knew the Bull of the Woods was capable of what he said.

By Monday morning at school, the sign on the fence was the talk of the school. I heard two students taking proud responsibility for the deed. Bobby and I kept quiet and I was pretty smug that one of these two fakes would take all the heat. At dinner that night, I even reported at the family meal the name of the boy who was bragging about it.

Unfortunately, this was not the end of the story. I assumed my brother Tom could keep a secret because I outweighed him by 40 pounds and was playing football. My assumptions were wrong, and I learned much later that he walked quietly into my mother's bedroom after dinner that night and said, "If you know something that is bad, should you tell on someone?" My mother didn't push him. She just said, "Tom, you need to think about it and ask Jesus what the right thing to do might be. You know that doing wrong things is always known by Him."

Tom has never shared with me how long he thought about it, but a few days later I had the conversation with my parents at which I broke down and told the truth about the fence. They asked me in a way that kept Tom out of it by simply stating that if I had done it, I really needed to get it off my chest. They did indicate that they were very concerned that Bobby and I had done it. I mean, they knew we were sleeping outside in September after school started. That certainly wasn't a usual pattern and he and I had never slept outside at the same time before. Probably my Dad had found the can of red paint.

The next day my father went with me to see the owner. I am pretty sure now that my father had already spoken to him. When I went through my confession, he stood up, his face got red and he boomed, "Do you realize, boy, what you have done to my reputation in this town? I will expect you and your friend to clean that fence off and pay for any repairs."

That was a difficult three days as each afternoon after school I could not go to football practice and Bobby and I were wire brushing, scraping and repainting the fence. It was only one block from the high school, so most of my friends walked by us while we worked. The temptation to be proud of our escapade just never materialized.

Oh, by the way, my father never whipped me within an inch of my life, and he did tell me that he was proud that I owned up to my mistake like a man. It was a lot later in my life before I forgave my brother when my mother finally told me that Tom had told on me.

❦

Every man carries baggage from his youth. The stories above are not as difficult as other men's stories of abuse, neglect and trauma. The illustrations are to help men process that we are the result of our younger-life experiences and, generationally, we are likely to repeat the same mistakes as our fathers.

The LORD is slow to anger, abounding in love and forgiving sin and rebellion. Yet he does not leave the guilty unpunished; he punishes the children for the sin of the fathers to the third and fourth generation (Numbers 14:18, NIV).

This passage indicates that there are generational behaviors and sin that are passed from father to son. I can't blame my father for my Bull of the Woods concept, but I will suffer consequences if I continue the behavior. As long as I harbor unforgiveness, or have a seared conscience in regard to my father, then I will continue in sin. And some of those sins will be the same things that he did.

❦

There is a legend at William Jewell College in Liberty, Missouri, where most of my family attended—grandparents, parents and siblings. The story is that some fraternity men led a cow all the way up the stairs in a four-story classroom building late one night in the early 1930s. The mess the next morning was a sight to behold. The perpetrators knew how difficult it is to lead a cow down stairs.

Thirty years later when I attended the same college, it was still an urban legend. Even years later, when I attended a college reunion, the legend of the cow in the building was still known by the students. A picture of the cow looking out of a fourth-floor window is a part of the college memorabilia. My father, who graduated from the college in 1933, told us that he had also heard of the legend and, though we frequently asked him if he knew who was responsible, he never admitted it during most of his life. But when he was 84 years old, and dying of cancer, he finally admitted to all of us at his final family reunion that he and another fraternity brother had indeed taken the cow into the building.

∽◌◌∾

I know these examples seem harmless, and after 70 years they probably are, but the reality that our quirks, behaviors and addictions and mistakes are passed to our children also apply in more substantial ways.

∽◌◌∾

Jerry came to see me when his wife discovered he had had an affair. He was remorseful, and it eventually came out in our sessions that his father, who was very wealthy, had many affairs himself. Jerry was financially in significant bondage to his father for help in some real estate deals he had made and he still owed his father money after more than 15 years. He always had to support his father's behavior when his wife would bring it up because, subconsciously, he could never denigrate his father since he owed him money. Although Jerry chose to have an affair, he had seared his conscience by not facing the sin in his father's life. Unfortunately, Jerry's mother was more forgiving and tolerant of the behavior than his own wife. His mother never left his dad, so Jerry thought his wife wouldn't leave him either. Although I encouraged

Jerry to forgive his father, admit his sin and arrange to get out of in-debtedness to him, Jerry couldn't do that. The bonds of generational sin are difficult to break. Today Jerry is divorced.

∽⌖∾

To bring all this together, we see that the suffering of broken gen-erational relationships is necessary to accomplish God's best in our marriage. Pain is designed to be a tool to let us know our deep life principles. The testing of our faith calls us to clear our conscience, and this improves the quality of our lives. Mourning means we rid ourselves of our past and our sinful thinking from a seared conscience. We can remove only the junk that we know is there, so God designs tests to bring the junk to our attention.

All of us have pain from relationships, and we need to pay atten-tion to what is hurting and clear our conscience. Like Paul, we keep short accounts.

We should always ask ourselves when we see the toilet seat down, "Did I leave it down; did I use it; where does she want it; did the boys use it; is it clean?" Then repent, if necessary; request forgiveness, make restitution, make a change. Trust me on this one; she complains when you leave it down and then use it standing up.

9

Discipleship in Marriage

In the long run wives are to be paid in a peculiar coin - consideration for their feelings. As it usually turns out this is an enormous, unthinkable inflation few men will remit, or if they will, only with a sense of being overcharged.

Elizabeth Hardwick, Seduction and Betrayal, 1974

There is probably no more confusion in men than the confusion that surrounds these verses:

> *Husbands, love your wives, just as Christ also loved the church and gave Himself for it, that He might sanctify and cleanse it with the washing of water by the word, that He might present it to Himself a glorious church, not having spot or wrinkle or any such thing, but that she should be holy and without blemish* (Ephesians 5:25–27, NKJV).

I believe that what a man needs to sacrifice is his male-dominant thinking. He doesn't give up being a male any more than by dying Christ gave up being God. The sacrifice is to stop thinking only male and think female. Now we should see what sanctify means.

What does that mean to sanctify her? Isn't sanctification of believers the work of the Holy Spirit in them and their obedience to it? Christ gave Himself for the church that He might sanctify it. Matthew Henry's commentary explains it this way, "That he might endue all his members with a principle of holiness and deliver them from the guilt, the pollution and the dominion of sin." (33. Henry)

Thus a man is called by God to a higher purpose of sanctifying his wife. While the Holy Spirit is the power for submission, the husband is a vehicle through which the grace of God flows into a woman's life. To sanctify our wives means we create an environment of developing holiness, meaning living without self-righteousness under the moment-by-moment guidance of the Holy Spirit. Living without any self-righteousness or expectations from others is the essence of sanctification. It is a life of not only self-denial and submission but of following God's leading all the time.

Men need to understand that the reason they develop this skill is to put their wives in a position where they will optimize the power of God in their lives. In the last century, marriage has made a profound change. As discussed in Chapter Five, there may be some good news in this process since women are abandoning the feminist movement and learning the blessings of the biblical concept of submission. Women need to be able to nurture and see male leadership and sacrifice.

Jesus spoke directly to this principle when He said:

Blessed are the meek, for they will inherit the earth (Matt. 5:5, NIV).

Meekness is not translated weakness. The New Living Translation translates meekness as gentle and lowly, but that doesn't capture all that I think it really means. The Greek word is *proates*, which means the possession of great power but having that power under control so that it is not used. It fits a picture of humility being displayed in a powerful king. It is like a president who is sensitive to the smallest need of another person. The meek person is not lowly of station by nature or birth, but by choice, knowing that he has the power to control his life but gives it up to follow God.

The meek are those who have subjected their will, their rights, their expectations, their goals, their plans and everything they are capable of accomplishing, in submission to the Holy Spirit. They have placed their choices under the control of the Holy Spirit. For the husband, this means that while he has all the power to control, to lord it over his wife, to demand obedience and submission, to expect her to meet all his needs, he does not stand on that right. He simply does not behave in that way. Real men are meek.

It's So Hard When You Know You're Right

In his book *Help, I'm Hurting*, Dr. Bill Oswalt explains that all of our problems are rooted in a right or expectation that we believe we have. We will build our own authority system, set ourselves up as king, develop a self-centered righteous anger and turn to the world for fulfillment. When someone eventually doesn't meet our expectation, we are pretty well hung out to dry. (29. Oswalt)

I suspect all of us have realized this self-centered system has caused significant relational problems and personal emotional pain. God gives us the problems and pain to point out this self-righteous character defect in us. In fact, Paul went to great length in teaching the Corinthians the hazards of these rights and expectations when he said:

> *Therefore concerning the eating of things offered to idols, we know that an idol is nothing in the world, and that there is no other God but one. For even if there are so-called gods, whether in heaven or on earth (as there are many gods and many lords), yet for us there is one God, the Father, of whom are all things, and we for Him; and one Lord Jesus Christ, through whom are all things and through whom we live.*
>
> *However, there is not in everyone that knowledge; for some, with consciousness of the idol, until now eat it as a thing offered to an idol; and their conscience, being weak, is defiled. But food does*

not commend us to God; for neither if we eat are we the better, nor if we do not eat are we the worse.

But beware lest somehow this liberty of yours become a stumbling block to those who are weak. For if anyone sees you who have knowledge eating in an idol's temple, will not the conscience of him who is weak be emboldened to eat those things offered to idols? And because of your knowledge shall the weak brother perish, for whom Christ died? (1 Cor. 8:4–11, NKJV)

He was speaking about the Corinthian Christians who no longer had to follow the Mosaic Law and avoid eating meat sacrificed to idols, but this behavior was having a significant effect on other less-mature believers.

How is it that God has given us desires and intelligence yet He tells us not to take the authority over our lives? All authority is given to Christ (Matthew 29:19); therefore, all rights and power are His. What this means to me is that I have no rights, authority or power. The really interesting thing is that His Word tells us that even though we have no rights, we have responsibilities.

But when you thus sin against the brethren, and wound their weak conscience, you sin against Christ. Therefore, if food makes my brother stumble, I will never again eat meat, lest I make my brother stumble (1 Cor. 8:12–13, NKJV).

Therefore do not let sin reign in your mortal body so that you obey its evil desires. Do not offer the parts of your body to sin, as instruments of wickedness, but rather offer yourselves to God, as those who have been brought from death to life; and offer the parts of your body to him as instruments of righteousness…Don't you know that when you offer yourselves to someone to obey him as slaves, you are slaves to the one whom you obey—whether you are slaves to sin, which leads to death, or to obedience, which leads to righteousness? But thanks be to God that, though you used to be slaves to sin, you wholeheartedly obeyed the form of teaching to which you were entrusted. You have been set free from sin and have become slaves to righteousness (Rom 6:12–18, NIV).

Giving up our rights is extremely difficult, particularly since we are convinced in our nature that we are right. Believing we are right, and being full of pride, is the very antithesis of humility and meekness. The choice is to yield to God.

Personally, I find this really tough to do. I am an intelligent guy and have gotten it right pretty much most of my life; so when I come up against a problem that really is a project God has given me, I can feel guilty if I fail. I have enough trouble working on myself let alone trying to take some responsibility for the sanctification of my wife. It would be easy for me just to work on myself and let her fix her own problems.

Well, that isn't what God's plan says. I don't have a right to just my own body but to that of my wife as well. Yes, we do need to get it together for our self, but then we have to look elsewhere for our next project.

The Emotional Work of Husbands

The next project will be involved with emotional responsiveness and the task of sanctification of our wives.

W. Bradford Wilcox, a sociologist from the University of Virginia, utilized the data from the U.S. Department of Health and Human Services Survey to evaluate various marriage model theories and the degree of marital happiness. His analysis discovered that the highest degree of marital happiness among all sorts of people was in those whose relationships were characterized by a high degree of emotional work by the husband in a marriage of the traditional model. The emotional work of the man in Wilcox's study is defined as any effort to express positive emotion to their wives, to be attentive to the dynamics of their relationship and the needs of their wives, or to set aside time for activities focused specifically on developing their relationship. Wilcox says:

Our findings also speak to the role of emotion work in women's global marital quality. First, it is important to highlight our finding, judging by the dramatic increase in model fit, that men's emotion work (and women's assessments of that work) is the most crucial determinant of women's marital quality. It is more important than patterns of household labor, perceptions of housework equity, female labor force participation, childbearing, education and a host of other traditional predictors of global marital quality. This finding suggests that the functions, character and stability of contemporary marriages are intimately tied to their emotional well-being. (34. Wilcox)

Dr. Wilcox notes that marriage research suggests the primary determinant of marital quality is the emotional character of the marriage. Women have long borne the primary emotional burdens of family life, and they are patterned in childhood toward proficiency in the emotional dynamics in relationships. Today other traditional sources of marital satisfaction have declined, like the acceptance of the homemaker model, the nonworking woman, higher rates of marital infidelity and absent husbands. As a result, women now place a premium on the emotional quality of their marriages that outweighs other sources of marital satisfaction. For the average American marriage, it matters a lot more whether the husband is emotionally in tune with his wife than whether he's doing, say, half the dishes or half the laundry. If the wife had to choose between having a husband who is taking half the housework and having a husband who is really making a conscious, deliberate effort to focus emotionally on his wife, the emotional focus is much more likely to be a paramount concern. (34. Wilcox)

So what is this emotional focus that a man must adopt? The apostle Paul told us to *sanctify and cleanse her with the washing of water by the word.* Sanctification means to set aside, to be made holy, without blemish, perfected, viewed by God as of inestimable value and meaning. Cleansed means she appears renewed, washed, as if she rose up from a baptism. The word is God's instructions to His children. The husband knows it well enough to use it to disciple his wife. If men are to have an emotional relationship with their wives they will have to be transparent, working on their blemishes and value before God. They will want to be prayed up and washed clean by the baptism of the word. Then as they do the emotional work in their relationship, they are reckoning themselves dead to the power of their own righteousness and yielded to His will for both their own lives and that of their wives.

Fred Littauer, in his book *Wake Up Men*, states, "Husbands are to become so Christlike that, through the process and the journey of the marital union with us, our wives will become spotless and wrinkle-free." We are to create such an atmosphere in the marriage that our wives will be seen by the Lord as holy and blameless. This does not imply that the wife has no responsibility of her own to reach for these objectives. She surely does. The verse is speaking only of our responsibility as husbands before the Lord. This means continuing our spiritual growth and maturity. (35. Littauer)

Discipleship means following a system of logic. Littauer says that men determine today what their spiritual future will be. Following God's system of growth logic will make us disciples of Christ. When we recognize a sin in our life, we already learned in Chapter Eight about confession and forgiveness in order to clear our conscience. In a man's discipleship growth, when he has cleared his conscience, the next phase involves looking at the rights, power, pride, intellect or agenda that he has that have gotten him into trouble. We turn it all over to God because He is the one with all authority. At the same time that we are giving up our rights, we are losing our expectations related to them.

The emotional focus that men must adopt is to give up our old system of logic which says, "I must control the tenor of the family; everyone must exist for me; I make the rules; I can't help the way I am, etc." As our personality and life experiences develop we set up patterns, beliefs and concepts about how things need to be in order to keep us in balance. These are our own sets of rules by which we live that will guarantee that we get what we want.

Confess Your Self-righteousness

So the first step in our personal transition is to confess any self-righteousness. When we do the hard work of sanctifying ourselves, we will have to stop putting ourselves first if we are going to have a spiritual relationship with our wives in order to sanctify them. If we are having relational troubles now, it is because our system of rules and beliefs are making our wives angry. We must stop trying to get her to accept our rules—and to find out what hers are.

Start now to make a fearlessly complete list of all the rights/rules that we have. Don't leave any out.

Do I have a right to have my wife ask for permission before making large purchases for Christmas gifts?

Do I have a right for her to take care of the maintenance schedule of her car because, after all, I am the one who works all day?

"What about a little sex tonight," when she gets home tired and late from a draining parent/teacher conference at school?

Here's one: "Honey, you can't disagree with me because I know more about that than you do."

Let Go of Being Right

Now that we have a list in our hands we should go somewhere and get in a quiet frame of mind and prayerfully give up all of our authority over all the issues. Just give them to God; they were all His to begin with. Write them down on a piece of paper and throw them into the fire or flush them away. Yes, I know we think a little sex would be a good deal tonight, but maybe we need to spend some time emotionally letting our wives unwind from the evening.

If we give up the system of behavioral logic that we have lived with in the past, we are sacrificing our self and we will find our self without an expectation to demand of someone else. With no expectations for behavior we have no conflict, because whatever someone does doesn't matter. Imagine how chaotic things can get if everyone is standing on their own right to do or believe a certain thing? The Israelites were often guilty of this, and God lost patience with them when they each did what they thought was right in their own eyes (see Judges 17:6).

Take Responsibility

Once we have given up our rules and regulations and have no agenda of expectations of our wives, God can fill us with the correct response to the situation we find ourselves involved in. God will give us the right response. It is then that God will give us the action that is our responsibility and we will need to take action on that responsibility.

The logic of discipleship in Christ is that everything men want to do or be, everything they think they deserve and everything that they are is subjected to the intense scrutiny of the Word of God. Since they are in a covenant relationship with a woman, i.e., they are married, they have a special calling to yield themselves to her and to lead her spiritual growth.

Here, one more time, are the steps to righteousness:

1. Confess self-righteousness
2. Make a list of personal rights.
3. Give the rights to God.
4. Give up your expectations.
5. Choose to take responsibility.
6. Prepare for a test. (29. Oswalt)

Jerry was getting concerned. Their credit-card bill each month had been more than he had money to pay and he was leaving some of it unpaid each month. Both he and his wife, Ruth, had come from a family where they pretty much got just about anything they wanted. They had both been working full time and owned their own home, with a big mortgage, and were driving two cars. They both wanted Ruth to spend most of her time at home for the first year or two after their son was born, but they had not been disciplined enough to slow the spending. Jerry was getting to the point where he hated the pain and suffering of trying to pay the bills and would become morose and procrastinate. Ruth would still spend money. Jerry was running out of new credit cards to open, and it was obviously affecting their marriage.

Jerry told me he loved his wife and son, hated his job and was depressed, thinking there was no way out. He resigned himself to climbing inside the television. He had a right for his wife to stop spending money and to go back to work. He had a right to feel down and to want to be left alone.

Ruth told me she loved her husband but hated how he was depressed and not taking responsibility for the home. She had a right to nice things for the house and pretty things for the baby, so she went back to her mother for consolation. All she wanted, she told me, was, "I wish he would share his pain with me, I hate it when he just stays out with his friends or sits in front of the TV."

When Paul and Terri made a move to a smaller town, they were excited because Paul's new job had sufficient income that Terri would not have to work. While their children were entering teenaged years, Terri was happy to have more time to be a soccer mom. Paul was hoping to have Terri adopt a stay-at-home mentality because she had been stressed out in her profession as a social worker in their previous hometown.

Both had always felt their life together was a competition. Paul was a class act of perfection, always leading the effort, always studiously striving to make everything all right. He had grown up in a competitive home and had always felt he was competing for affection and recognition from his father. He was a master at keeping Terri under his leadership. He couldn't possibly identify his character defect— that is, until he lost his job with the large company.

His was not in an emotional relationship with Terri. It was like he had to be with other men; his goal was to win, not to emote. Terri just had to suck it up and accept that she was imperfect, all the while seeing the imperfections in Paul. All Terri could say in our session was, "I wish he would just talk to me as a person and not as something he is trying to fix."

Both couples had come to Pat and me for help.

Jerry and Ruth's relationship was in crisis, but through counseling and financial planning they were able to get it back on track. But it had to start with Jerry. We pointed out that Jerry was standing on a right to have a reasonable boss, the payment of an appropriate bonus and a wife who would control her spending and quit wanting so many expensive things. He needed to confess his self-righteousness and need for space and give up the right that his wife be part of the solution. He also needed to give up the right to a decent boss and a fair shake at work.

The expectation of certain behaviors in his boss and wife were gone, and he could see a different reason why God might have him in that job and how he was going to have to learn a better financial discipline. He began to share himself with Ruth on an emotional level and became disciplined at working through his approach at work.

Paul and Terri were also in a financial crisis. As we discussed in Chapter Seven, we rarely find a couple in crisis that are not also in crisis with their finances. Finances are not always the cause of the problem, but a broken marriage is usually broken in finances that have to be fixed along with the other problems. Paul continued to talk with me as he took a lower-paying job and Terri had to go back to work for a period of time. He had trouble recognizing that his competitive approach and demands for performance toward his wife, children and the people he worked with was not how he was going to sanctify his wife or serve God in righteousness. He needed to be a partner together with his wife and help her achieve her goals and calling since now God had made it necessary for her to seek meaningful service work. Our sessions took some work to identify his compulsion-to-win characteristic and see it as a defect, but he did. He realized when he let go of the expectations he had, and related on an equal basis with his wife, his circumstances improved greatly

For both Jerry and Paul, the financial pressures brought them to their senses with their roles at home to disciple their wives. Neither was protecting his wife; the pressures of their situations were keeping them from being engaged emotionally with their wives. Their wives could see it; they even tried to talk with them about it, but their self-righteousness and pride would not let them see it.

Men who lord it over their wives will get simple acquiescence. Developing an emotionally vulnerable relationship will get them a powerful ally.

Dr. Wilcox notes, "The biggest predictor a of woman's happiness is her husband's emotional engagement. The extent to which he is affectionate, to which he is empathetic, to which he is basically tuned into his wife, is the most important factor in predicting the wife's happiness." (34. Wilcox)

I told Jerry and Paul that it did not matter how bad the financial situation was; all they needed was to focus on understanding their wives, searching for their needs and then emotionally engaging them in a transparent, vulnerable fashion. That means they unloaded their expectations, because if they could do that, they would be emotionally engaging and vulnerable.

Remember when the two wives said: "I wish Jerry would share his pain with me. I hate it when he just stays out with his friends and sits in front of the TV," and, "I wish Paul would just talk to me as a person and not as something he is trying to fix."

I believe the answer to these pleas by a wife is the sanctification that a man does by sacrificing himself and focusing on her. Every time a man emotionally engages his wife, she will move heaven and earth to solve whatever the problem is. In some way, neither Jerry nor Paul needed this great and wonderful plan for debt resolution, job change or a new job. What they needed was to engage their wives by sacrifice and setting her apart. Yes, they needed to get financial advice, remain responsible in their work and be involved around the house. Yet, being empathetic, affectionate and tuned in to her, engages power beyond either alone. It is a pretty picture to behold.

Make Me a Slave to the Righteous Response

Demonstrating meekness through the power of the Holy Spirit can sometimes seem overwhelming: The apostle Paul said, *I do not understand what I do. For what I want to do I do not do, but what I hate I do... So then, I myself in my mind am a slave to God's law, but in the sinful nature a slave to the law of sin* (Rom 7:15 and 25, NIV).

I have sat up late at night many times over my lifetime pondering Paul's words in Romans 6 and 7. More than any others, they have given me peace and purpose. I am a proud man, powerful in every way. I am taller, wealthier and brighter than 98 percent of Americans. I really do have trouble not boasting, expecting certain things and enjoying a high sense of entitlement. I wish I could say I curse being tall or rich or bright. I wish it were easy to not be all those things; then I could be humble. But I am all those things and I live with that curse. My challenge is to recognize all that power and subject it in submission to the grace of God.

I know that I struggle no more and no less than Paul did. I know that when we recognize that our sins/problems are rooted in an assumed right, we can confess this to God and give up all expectations. He will give us the ability to make the right response. Paul notes, *What a wretched man I am! Who will rescue me from this body of death? Thanks be to God—through Jesus Christ our Lord* (Rom. 7:24–25, NIV).

The Beatitudes of Christ carry with them a reward. The promised reward for the discipline that it takes to be sanctified or meek is that we shall inherit the earth. James Dillon, in his book *Reign of the Servant Kings*, discusses that this means those who are called to His purpose and are continually reckoning themselves dead to the power of their own righteousness, and are yielded to His, will grow in their responsibility and reign with Him in the New Jerusalem in the millennium; i.e., they actually inherit the Earth. (36. Dillow)

10

Primer on Human Sexuality
Savvy, seductive or sensitive

All men are fools and motivated by sex

Allan W. Windmiller

People who write books about couple relationships eventually have to get to the discussion of how things are going in the bedroom. I've been in men's ministry for many years and have been counseling men for more than 15 years. The matter of sex in marriage is not as complex as men might think and basically boils down to three issues. By obtaining honest answers to these three questions I can pretty much get a handle on what needs to be done in the marriage. We don't have to spend a lot of time on the subject; men can either grasp what I teach them or they can't. So here are the three questions I ask men:

1. Are you having sex because you want it or because you want to please her?
2. Who else are you having sex with or want to have sex with?
3. Are you addicted to pornography?

I know there is a lot more to sexuality than those three things. If men grasp everything else about understanding their wives and learn the correct three answers to those questions, they will do just fine. I am sure there are some really deep-seated emotional problems involving sexual child abuse or rape or significant sexual trauma from an earlier period that may require more specific sexuality counseling, but that is for another book or expert, not this one.

Just read Song of Solomon in order to understand that human sexuality is a biblical principal. The book is not an allegory of the relationship between a believer and his Christ or a picture of God's relationship with the Children of Israel. It is a beautiful poetic description of the love of Solomon and the Shulamite woman. This book is an affirmation of the physical relationship that springs out of a deep and abiding God-given love between two people.

It speaks to the principle that longing is a part of love. Never should I stop thinking of her. Actually, when love is true, I cannot—I must speak to her, of her, my thoughts are always with her. Neither can I lie down at night nor awaken in the morning without her face in my every thought.

For the Shulamite woman in the Song of Solomon:

- Love will not be silent.
- Spring and love go together. My lover said to me, "Rise up, my beloved, my fair one and come away. For the winter is past, and the rain is over and gone. The flowers are springing up, and the time of singing birds has come, even the cooing of turtledoves. The fig trees are budding, and the grapevines are in blossom. How delicious they smell! Yes, spring is here! Arise, my beloved, my fair one, and come away" (Song of Solomon 2:10–13, NLT).
- Love is exclusive. "My lover is mine, and I am his." (2:16)
- Love is enhanced by friendship. "His legs are like pillars of marble set in sockets of the finest gold, strong as the cedars of Lebanon. None can rival him. His mouth is altogether sweet;

he is lovely in every way. Such, O women of Jerusalem, is my lover, my friend." (5:15–16)

- Love sees only the beautiful. "My lover is dark and dazzling, better than ten thousand others" (5:10–11).
- Love involves giving and receiving.
- Love means risking and the possibility of pain, "Make this promise to me, O women of Jerusalem! If you find my beloved one, tell him that I am sick with love" (5:8). "One night, as I lay in bed, I yearned deeply for my lover, but he did not come" (3:1–2).
- Words fail in expressing love.
- Love must be given freely.
- True love is priceless.

So, in order to clear the stage about what God thinks about sex, let's look at some of the doctrinal truths gleaned from a careful look at the Bible. Clearly the story of creation and relationships between men and women in the Bible indicate:

- Man and woman complement each other in every way. We've already looked at how she fills the voids we have in our lives and personality, and we do the same for her.
- Man and woman are physically attracted to each other. That is obviously how God created us, since it leads to intimacy, pleasure and pregnancy.
- We are sexually suitable since we are to multiply and fill the earth.
- Although in today's world one may not get the idea of exclusivity in the relationship, human sexuality is to be expressed in an exclusive relationship. It works best in that way; a nonexclusive relationship is void of trust, full of jealousy and fear of abandonment.
- As for the techniques of sex and its pleasures, the standard would be that anything is permissible as long as it is desired by both partners and affords mutual pleasure.

Whom Are You Pleasing Here?

Ed and Gaye in their book *Intended for Pleasure*, regarding a Christian perspective on the fundamentals of human sexuality, note several things for men to think about if their sex life isn't what they really want it to be. Interviewing a large number of women has revealed that for the woman, the extent and depth of pleasure she finds in making love sexually flows out of her inner attitude about her husband. If we had a fight in the morning and haven't resolved it yet, don't expect her to respond to amorous advances that night. Yes, a woman might agree to sex because of a sense of duty rather than one of delight, and she will usually simply perform the duty rather than delight in the performance. Most women who are having regular sex with their hurry-up husband are not having an orgasm. A husband might want to ask his wife sometime about how often she does. (37. Wheat)

On the other hand, although men rate sex as pretty good if they have an orgasm, more careful development of the skills needed to please her will result in a man who rates sex as *outstanding* when he sees his wife excited and thrilled. Men find the depth of their pleasure flowing from visual and hormonal senses. Men like to watch during sex; women don't. The woman is enjoying the closeness and interaction verbally and the touching with her husband. We should talk with her, listen to her and respond, say sweet things that we really mean and, for goodness' sake, we don't make love after sweating all day at work or just after a work-out. Be attractive for her.

It really is true that women want to be treated like a queen. Does she know that she is the single most important person in her husband's life? Next to God, do we want to please her the most? Sexually and physically, do we accept our wife the way she is or are we trying to make her be some sex animal that she isn't? Most of us are a little overweight, don't have a chiseled body and could never pass for a model, so we ought not to make her feel like less of a woman by trying to dress her up in skimpy lingerie.

Sexual responses are not automatically released. Communication of pleasure during sex is important, even nonverbal activity like hand guiding. It is important to find out what she needs to become excited and to try approaches by asking her, "Do you like that?" Preparation and comfort will really let the sex juices flow and ensure that she is comfortable, not having her head banging against the headboard and ensuring there is either natural or synthetic lubrication. Keep the slick juice in the bed stand, ready for action.

Good sex is a must for a good marriage. If either mate is dissatisfied, it's a major issue. I have never counseled a couple who had problems big enough to seek counseling who didn't have significant sexual displeasure. Now I am not saying that sexual displeasure is the cause of all marital discord; what I am saying is that all marital discord has a piece of sexual dysfunction.

Oneness in Sex Reinforces Oneness in Every Other Aspect of the Marriage.

A man can't be having sex with two or more women and still have an intimate, meaningful relationship with his wife as God designed it. It just doesn't work. I've had Christian men tell me that it was possible, that they could fall into bed with other women, even another woman in their church, and it would have no effect on their wives. Since God didn't design men to sleep with everyone, unlike the bull in the cattle yard, there must be consequences from such behavior.

From my experiences in counseling, I see men in broken marital relationships who slip into bed with other women because their wives have gone frigid on them or can't meet their needs. So they need to get serviced somewhere else. If a man were to obtain sexual satisfaction from his wife, there would be no need to stray. A straying man has a guilty conscience, and that guilt will affect his intimacy with his wife; it is not possible to separate the two. The adulterous man has been so selfish in his sexual needs that he has not taken pleasure in ensuring that his wife enjoys what he so much enjoys because he hasn't got a clue how to please her, and if he is getting it somewhere else, he has no urge to learn how to please his wife.

I believe that a failure to love our wives in all of the ways we've been talking about throughout this book, failing to understand her need for emotional responsiveness, intimacy and security, will reduce her satisfaction with sex. Because of non-communication, inability to emotionally respond to his wife or being unable to fill her needs, some men understand that their marriage relationship has broken down and has caused their sexual relationship and mutual pleasure to wane. They have to go out to get serviced because their hormones are just driving them crazy. As the marriage is crashing from any number of possibilities, the man usually wanders. Less commonly, sometimes it is the woman.

When there has been a waning of sexual satisfaction or wandering, it has to be faced head on. One partner may be guilty of failing to satisfy the other partner and/or actually straying from the relationship. In either case there will need to be healing. The partner who has been sexually unfaithful will need to repent, go to the other, confess the wrong and desire to start anew. But before we amplify this resolution, let's talk about the third question

Artificial Sex—Pornography and the World's Fascination with Lust

Lust is defined as obsessive or excessive thoughts or desires of a sexual nature. Unfulfilled lust sometimes leads to sexual or sociological compulsions and/or transgressions including, but not limited to, sexual addiction, adultery and, in even less common circumstances, rape. Dante Alighieri in his epic poem *The Divine Comedy*, considered lust as desire gone excessive. (38. Alighieri) The immodesty of the American culture has established a focus on sexual matters that is a colossal temptation to men. The ease with which one's fantasies of a sexual nature can be fed from immodest dressing, television, movies and the internet means that even the most assiduous man of honor may find himself falling into temptation. We may have no intention of looking, but it is in front of us at such an incredible scale that we might fail. A real man guards against this; he guards his mind and considers a second or longer look as a slam at his wife. Remember that she is the love of our life, not the nameless body we just saw.

Other men are senseless about the subject and some actually want their wives to look at pornographic material with them as a form or excitement. Real men don't do that; they know that looking at pornography is not a turn-on for a woman.

What is happening in the world is still more subtle than simply the pornographic problem. The minimization of the importance of the Christian idealized view of sex has done much to trivialize the importance and value of sexuality in marriage. It has been going on in the media for years and has finally become the norm in the adolescent world. Hopping into bed is a part of the culture of couple relationships, a right of adolescent passage, and it is described by teenagers in terms of the physiology of desire and enjoyment that is a normal part of growing into physical maturity. It is rarely ever discussed in terms of marital commitment. Fully three-fourths of high school-graduating men and sixty percent of women have had sex. Most adolescents can describe in great detail how to put on a condom and the physiology of the sex act and how to do it, but haven't got a clue about the intimacy of a personal relationship forever with a wife, including the inestimable value of the one-on-one commitment to each other.

This view of sex is what characterized Dante's description of the punishment in the second circle of hell where the consequences of lust are dealt with.

> "Those overcome by lust are punished in this circle. They are the first ones to be truly punished in Hell. These souls are blown about to and fro by a violent storm, without hope of rest." (38. Alighieri)

This symbolizes the power of lust to blow one about needlessly and aimlessly. Men who have ever had a pornographic, wanton sexuality or adultery problem know exactly what Dante meant about being blown to and fro by the desire of pleasure of pictures or movies, or the tingling excitement of an adulterous affair, conflicted against the desire to be faithful to their wives.

But the man who commits adultery is an utter fool, for he destroys his own soul (Prov. 6:32, NLT).

I know it is not easy to get out of this situation and to achieve a new look at a marriage. Men with this problem will need to realize how devastating this sort of behavior is toward their wives. Of course a man needs to repent, confess the wrong to her and ask for her forgiveness. Having a band of brothers who will hold him accountable to purity is a requisite for any success in staying clean.

There is a strong recommendation that counselors generally make in severe situations. When use of pornography or a sexual affair has been discovered, and the man has repented and returned to the spouse for forgiveness, counselors recommend that the return to sexual intimacy does not immediately occur. There needs to be a period of physical separation for the hurt to heal. The length of time is not defined. The man will need to reestablish trust, redevelop a friendship that includes dating his wife and wait for the responsiveness of his wife to demonstrate she is ready for more intimacy. Furthermore, in the instance of an extramarital affair where each is committed to reconciliation, the man must not ever have any contact whatsoever with the other lover or the pornographic material. It is as if it is a drug or alcohol, and only abstinence will work.

Making It Happen in Bed—Please Her

I would like to make some concise recommendations to men who are sure they want to please their wives as the primary function of sex and desire a few simple reminders to assist them to reach that goal. These will be helpful to a young man just married or a man married many years.

Sexual pleasure should be more than just spontaneous. A man ought to look ahead and anticipate what he might say, do, wear or be to show her that he is thinking about her. Some time spent planning how it might be later that day or night, and some signal that it is on his mind, will reap great rewards.

Talk to each other, listen to each other and respond verbally to each other. Talk about fun things, pleasant things and dream together. Read poetry, pray together and share thoughts.

Make sex a priority. Remove distractions. Lock the door and be sure the kids are in bed. When it is over, don't just roll over and go to sleep or jump out of bed to the shower. Cuddle her, stay with her during the slow decline of the afterglow.

There needs to be a leader and a follower in the whole affair. Most times it is the man, and the initiation of the tempo and the events and the progress of the affair are like an orchestra being directed by the man. If the woman enjoys an on-top position, let her select it and enjoy it. Once in a while she might even like directing.

Just as with an orchestra, each one has a melody to play, a part to perform; between a man and his wife wonderful, enjoyable music can be played. Great love comes when each one has achieved maximum enjoyment.

A man and a woman should present themselves to the other as a precious gift. The situation should be set up as to maximize positive effects on all the senses. For the man, he should be clean and, if his wife doesn't like beards or stubble, he should be clean shaven. The morning breath or halitosis should be dealt with by a breath mint or a toothbrush. Just a whiff of a favorite cologne or perfume would be appropriate. I will never forget one Valentine's day when I came out of the bathroom into the bedroom filled with a dozen red candles, Pat lying naked and curled like a coquet on the white sheets and the entire bed covered with rose petals.

Exploring all variations of the love-making act through verbal and nonverbal means can enhance the experience. Search for areas of stimulation, positions of pleasure for variety and share what pleasures they bring. Guiding her hand and suggesting or correcting will give her permission to do the same to you in order to maximize pleasure.

Kathleen Parker writes that men who regularly help women reach orgasm are in some combination more empathetic, fonder of their partner, emotionally savvier and perhaps better seducers. These characteristics are attractive to women. Parker indicates that these men also make better fathers, are more likely to raise children successfully. Seductiveness may attract partners, but is not necessarily associated with good child-rearing skills. What men need to gain is emotional skill, since that is what she is looking for. It turns out that men who are better lovers produce savvier and more sensitive human beings. (10. Parker)

Seventy-year-olds who are still sexually active within a long-term relationship display certain characteristics about their relationship: They express their love verbally. They are physically affectionate. They express their love through sexuality. They express appreciation and admiration. They are mutually transparent to each other. They are best friends. They express love materially with gifts and tasks. They accept demands and put up with shortcomings. They create time to be alone together.

Finally, in the area of sexuality, we need to remember the words of Paul:

> *The husband should not deprive his wife of sexual intimacy, which is her right as a married woman, nor should the wife deprive her husband. The wife gives authority over her body to her husband, and the husband also gives authority over his body to his wife* (1 Cor. 7:3–4, NLT).

This is an often-misunderstood verse and most people, particularly women, take it to mean they have to just lie there and let the man service himself. What Paul is talking about is primarily emphasizing the man's role in pleasing his wife through sexual expression. When she is just being the servicing partner, her husband is cheating her of normal sexual relations in favor of his selfishness. Paul notes that the woman has a right for the man to please her in sexuality, and his failure to do so is wrong.

11

Reaching the High Sacred Ground
of Manhood

"There's no such thing as legacies. At least, there is a legacy, but I'll never see it."

George W. Bush

As I was reading John Eldredge's book *Wild at Heart*, I was continually struck by the God-given desire in every man to have an adventure. (2. Eldredge)

I recently spent a week with my three-and-a-half year old grandson. We would go for walks, ride bikes in the park or just play around with his cars. One morning, when I asked him what he wanted to do, he said, "I want to look for treasure." He wanted an adventure to go on. I had to bury it and then give him clues to find it. And I couldn't just bury an old ball; it had to be real money—and big pieces of money. I think I have a budding Indiana Jones on my hands.

We wouldn't just ride bicycles for exercise or transportation; it was a race. "Opa," he'd say, "You catch me now." The sidewalk we were on was intermittently narrowed by trees, and at one juncture he tried to pass me on the right just as we came to a narrowing. I heard him coming and felt him bump into me, causing me to veer into the hedge-row. I bounced off of it and fell into him, knocking us both to the ground. He bounced his head (with a helmet on) on the tire of a car parked at the curb. Of course he screamed loudly. A quick evaluation led me to know that he was all right and while he was sobbing uncontrollably I said, "Asher, you're all right; you just can't pass Opa when it's too narrow."

Well, he instantly stopped sobbing, laughed and said, "I'm okay, I'm okay; let's get home. I'm sorry, Opa." He knew he had caused the accident. He was learning that an adventure involves risk. Asher is just beginning the great adventure of life. According to Eldredge, adventure is what God sets a man to do in life.

As for me, well, now I am an older man. I have two metal hips and some chronic arthritis, and it isn't as easy to get up and go. I received my first Social Security check a while ago, but I still go hiking or snow-shoeing with some adventure in mind. "I wonder where this is leading. I wonder if I could get to that hillside in the winter to ski down it in the powder." When I found an abandoned mine shaft during one hike, I was ecstatic. "Here's something to explore."

But I know I don't have unlimited time left and I am very happy with this phase of life which can best be described as reaching the higher sacred ground of life. With some considerable soul searching and wise counsel, many years ago I set out to define this sacred ground which characterizes this end of my life. Watching it come into fruition is a joy in itself. There aren't many things left in the world for me to do. I've done multistage-sport rock climbing as lead, I've been head of large business institutions, and I've raised three sons, living through the death of one of them. I have skied the deepest powder, broken bones in sports and won trophies and medals. I've tried and mastered new techniques in my profession and have been a teacher with an endowed associate professor-of-medicine chair. I spent over ten years as an elder in three different churches. I have also published a book.

But all of those accomplishments will not matter someday. Today they matter only to me; they don't matter to others. I suppose they might matter to my children and grandchildren. But when my health really starts to fail, and I grow closer to the glory of departing from this life, those accomplishments will stop mattering even to me. Whatever it is that will matter must matter for us for all eternity. When I attended men's fraternity seminars, the later sessions involved an exercise in writing the plans for the rest of our lives. Robert Lewis notes, "A real adventurer will first carefully define this sacred ground of the rest of his life and then wisely navigate his life with these ends in mind." It involves what we want to leave behind, and what we leave behind is not a list of our accomplishments. So what do we want to leave behind? What do we want to be remembered for?

There are two ways to go through life:

- **The reactive life.** This one consists of comparing my life to others and competing. It produces unhealthy pressures in a man.

  The proactive life. This one consists of envisioning my life and enjoying putting it together wildly. It produces healthy pursuits. (5. Lewis)

John Eldredge puts another spin on it when he notes: "Don't ask yourself what the world needs—just commit to something. What the world needs are committed men." (2. Eldredge) The recent movie, *Bucket List*, was a powerful reminder of envisioning what we want to end up like and what we want to be, to do or to experience. Morgan Freeman and Jack Nicholson take a journey into things they had never done before when they discover that they are both terminally ill. They determine together to accomplish a few things before they "Kick the Bucket." The main lesson from the movie is the importance of healing or keeping relationships healthy, not just sky-diving or riding a motorcycle on the Great Wall of China.

My brother has always kept a list of what he wants to do or experience in this life and is diligent to stay after it. One thing that was on his list was a trek in New Zealand. He did it with a friend and even enjoyed tea with Sir Edmund Hilary about a year before Hilary's death. Another thing on his annual list is watching the annual Colorado State High School basketball championships all in one weekend, or one of the regional NCAA playoffs of March Madness. The important lesson here is that we must have a plan and a framework from which we are directed, because if we don't, what Henry David Thoreau noted will haunt us as we age: "Most men lead lives of quiet desperation and go to the grave with the song still in them." (15. Thoreau)

Ever since I was a boy, I had always wanted to have a little place in the mountains to live in when it snows. I was envious of those people who spend a whole year alone in a cabin in the woods. Pat and I purchased a small log cabin on two acres of pine forest adjacent to the national forest. It was a second home for us for four years. We added a master bedroom suite and game room to it and used it as a getaway place. In the fall of 2007, I convinced her that we weren't getting any younger and now was the time to move ourselves to the cabin to see if we could survive in it as our only home. It is perched on a ridge with a view of mountain peaks and miles and miles of forest, a half an hour from town and the hospital where I work. Quiet and simply beautiful, it provides serenity of great joy when we slip up there for a few days each month.

Living the adventure every single day has proven to be a quite different matter. First of all, we now have a daily commute of an hour. And the first winter that we chose to stay all winter broke the all-time record for total snowfall, over 500 inches in the Park Range in northwestern Colorado where the average is 250 inches. The adventure for us was learning how to live for 30 straight days where it snowed an average of three to five inches each day—every single day—day after day. Shoveling snow was not what I thought would make the biggest impression on me while living in a cool cabin. I was developing a life of quiet desperation while I lived the dream. But at least that song of living in a snowy cabin was being sung before I went to the grave.

I can guarantee that during that winter I scoped out the location near my mountain cabin where a long aspen glade of powder-skiing exists. Amazingly enough I actually skied the route on the second of May.

Pat has been really great about understanding this longing in me for adventure. Women don't easily understand what seems like "useless activity." It is essential to a man; we must have an adventure. It is what keeps us energized and recharged to go forth with all the other responsibilities of manhood. Not every dream will turn out the way we thought, but God put us in that circumstance and it is something we planned to do in our lives. So whatever happens must be by God's design. We haven't lost by trying a thing; we can only lose by not trying at all. Nevertheless, we still need to be adventurous within the confines of the best advice of our wives.

Success is the happy feeling we get between the time we do something and the time we tell a woman what we did.

We Need to Finish Strong

We need to finish life strong. A man needs to get it right as he grows old together with his wife. God does have a plan for the game of life, and only we can play that game. Below is a starting place for each man to plan for the future.

What we start now will be our legacy. Legacy means, 1) property bequeathed to someone in a will, 2) something tangible inherited from a predecessor, 3) some intangible heritage passed on. Interestingly enough, the term legacy is used in the educational and fraternal realm to mean we may be recruited to a college, fraternity or sorority simply because our parents attended. In each case above, something passes to us from someone else, tangible or intangible. We've already discussed that our accomplishments will not matter; we can't pass them on. A spirit of adventure can be passed on and a spirit of manhood can be passed on. Every man needs a work to do, a will to obey and a woman to love. How well we do this is vital to who we will become and what we will leave because we will have an impact and will leave a legacy with people. Etienne Gilson said, "History is the only laboratory we have in which to test the consequences of thought." Don't forget

Winston Churchill's famous history quote, "History will be kind to me for I intend to write it." Using the outline below as suggested by Lewis is a way to write our history so that when it happens, it will be kind to us. (5. Lewis)

Before I die I want to:

BE: _____

DO: _____

HAVE: _____

HELP: _____

ENJOY: _____

LEAVE: _____

It could be a "Bucket List," like Freeman and Nicholson came up with, and we could fill it with things or tasks like this:

Before I die I want to:

Be a scratch golfer.

Do something really dangerous like sky-diving.

Take a trip to the South Pole.

Help my children gain financial independence.

Enjoy a vacation in Tuscany with my wife.

Leave half my estate to my college.

There is nothing wrong with that list and it could well motivate us to get committed to some planning and golf driving-range practice, but I would ask, "Will it get me to a higher plane spiritually or into a better relationship with my wife? Will it leave a heritage?"

Here is another set of thoughts that initially might seem like they are really godly:

Before I die, I want to:

Be known as a godly man.

Do whatever the Lord puts in my path.

Have a powerful daily prayer life.

Help people in my church grow in discipleship maturity.
Enjoy studying God's Word.
Leave a legacy of godly wisdom to those who know me.

See how hollow even these lofty ideas sound when confronted with the reality that most of us aren't looking daily for what God puts in our path? We don't pray without ceasing or help our brothers and sisters in Christ grow spiritually. I guess I might consider Billy Graham as having achieved those lofty goals, but how many of us is a Billy Graham. I'm lucky if I take time to read my Bible twice a week.

If a man is working to resolve difficulties and to understand his wife, he really needs to finish this last chapter strong with action steps for the rest of his life. That man's list could be relative to his wife's relationships and his newfound awareness, something like this:

Before I die I want to:

Be a warrior for my wife; one on whom she can depend.
Do something, instead of just standing and staring blankly when I am confronted with a character defect.
Have a watershed discussion with another man about my life wounds.
Help my wife to feel secure through solid financial planning and budgeting.
Enjoy sharing the experiences of life with my wife through conversation.
Leave no stone of wrong thinking unturned in coming to a new way of thinking about marriage.

Living with a list like that could change a man's life.

Here's some other guidance about working on life lists like these. When a man looks to develop an adventurer's life plan, the characteristics of this important project may include some or all of the following:

- Proactively craft the adventure rather than wandering through life, even if life is presently a success. This is really important.

Not only do some men live lives of quiet desperation and die with the song still in them, a few men live lives of success that just seem to have come to them, and they seem happy and content only to come to the end empty and wondering if it all amounted to anything. The principle, Carpe Diem, comes to mind here.

- Dreams should be realistic but not restrictive. Here's an example: winning a marathon is not realistic; planning to run one might be. I realistically cannot form my wife into a movie star by my love and attention, but she may become a role model to younger women, and she can teach them personal skills that may move some of them into such a position.

- Find someone to help you dream. A wife is a good one to find, but men also need men to help them dream—primarily men's dreams.

- It's never too late to start an adventure. Wisdom and experience are great sharpeners to adventure since maturity makes us focus more and develop a picture of an adventure. I have in mind a 400-foot rock spire that I am going to climb before my 75th birthday. But I have to find a guide, a belayer, get permission from the property owner and set a date.

- Young men will need to dream first-half-of-life dreams primarily. Youth have fire; they are invincible. They won't yet need to plan where they will retire and what they'll teach their grandchildren. What they need is a fight to live through. They will compete, even if it is against their own personal bests. Setting plans for younger children and meaningful experiences they can do with their wives should be their focus. Some plans will be with men if their wife doesn't enjoy tent-camping, yet he should still plan something with the more genteel wife. When we were younger, Pat's idea of camping was staying at the Lake Louise Lodge while I went kayaking on the Bow River. I was able to convince her once to be my belayer on a rock climb. One of the requirements for a belayer is to look at the climber.

Pat didn't like the idea that I even climbed, let alone liking to look at me clinging to a rock wall.

- The younger we start this proactive process, the greater the return of reward, adventure and nobility rather than regret. This process should be done every year. Watch what we've done in the last year relative to our planning and then plan where it will go in the next year. The list will evolve.

- Real men start with a draft and finish with a solid plan. Real men will keep polishing this project. (5. Lewis)

I have put lists and timelines together since I was 35 years old. Lists will change, and mine were no exception. I remember one of my items was to be promoted to Brigadier General in the Air Force. I planned the route, obtained the appropriate training, assignments and mentors and performed well. Little did I know that God had other plans. Our son Brett's life became a crisis for our family on a timeline, just as my General-officership timeline became a reality. The day I was notified by the Surgeon General that I was to be relocated and promoted, I had a crisis between my planning and observing God's will. Pat and I discussed the effect on our family. As we explored the ramifications of a move over 2,000 miles from where Brett was settled and where our support structure was located, I realized that relocating would result in severe dysfunction in his life and ours. Though it had been a dream for 15 years, I turned down the promotion. My mentor was incredulous. I don't think many officers ever turn down a promotion to be a flag officer. Making that decision did not give me a sense of reward and adventure for a new life in the senior Air Force officer ranks; it did, however, build in me a sense of nobility. Doing the noble thing removes the possibility of regret. Regret never follows making the right decision. That's how a man knows it is right.

I might share some of my thoughts as I considered the set up for the end of my life. Before I die, I want to:

- Be responsive from my loving heart and strength for the needs of my wife, children and grandchildren
- Do whatever it takes to have a regular interaction with my sons and grandchildren in a spiritual-mentor role
- Have a daily interaction of substance with my wife.
- Help men grow in the responsibility of loving their wives by teaching, counseling and personal example.
- Enjoy counseling couples in conjunction with my wife and not be afraid to speak the truth in love.
- When I depart, leave behind a people who will believe in God's plan for His church and be committed to it in reaching the community in which they live.

If I ever meet you after you have read this book, I'll ask you some questions:

- In a disagreement, which is your goal: to understand her feelings and input or to ensure she understands yours?
- What do you say to a woman in order to understand her?
- What does sacrifice look like to you in relation to your wife?
- When and how should you express your feelings?
- Before you die, what do you want? Is it written down?
- Reflect on how you would use the toilet seat, up or down.

Epilogue

My prayer is that men will enjoy the benefits of a godly marriage. If my journey has helped, then I have modeled what William Penn wrote: "I expect to pass through life but once. If, therefore, there be any kindness I can show, or any good thing I can do to any fellow being, let me do it now and not defer or neglect it, as I shall not pass this way again."

I recently saw the fighter pilot who wanted me to fix his wife, the one whom I mentioned in the introduction. It was at a 526th Fighter Squadron reunion, and I thanked him for the experience with his wife, explaining that it started me and my wife on a long journey of growing together and it produced a ministry in churches that we do helping couples in marital crisis. He told me, "Well, Doc, it turns out she wasn't fixable, but I have been married to a Christian woman for 20 years now, and we are very happy together." He thanked me for telling him the story of my journey.

Finally, my father did teach me one of the most lasting lessons of my marriage. This is a very valuable lesson and I believe we can tell a lot about the depth to which a man has grown in understanding his wife by how he manages this small area of his relationship. My father always told me that I should always sit down when using the toilet to pee. I do not know if he told the same thing to my brothers. Apparently he and my mother had words about how the four boys between the ages of 5 and 13 were spraying a space five feet in diameter around the toilets in the house. My father painted for me a very clear picture of the pleasure a woman gets cleaning toilets or when she sits, only to discover a wet seat.

REAL MEN UNDERSTAND THEIR WIVES

Real men who understand their wives will follow this advice: Leave the toilet seat down. That's where she wants it. Only use the seat by sitting or kneeling because the seat will always be where she is happiest. After all, it is called a throne. And never miss, or splash.

References Cited

1. Feirstein, Bruce, *Real Men Don't Eat Quiche*, New English Library, Ltd, London, 1982.
2. Eldredge, John, *Wild at Heart: Discovering the secret of a man's soul*, Thomas Nelson, Inc., Nashville TN, 2001.
3. Murrow, David, *Why Men Hate Going to Church*, Thomas Nelson, Inc., Nashville TN, 2005.
4. Coughlin, Paul, *No More Christian Nice Guy, When being nice—instead of good—hurts men, women and children*, Bethany House, Minneapolis, MN 2005.
5. Lewis, Robert, *Men's Fraternity: The Quest for Authentic Manhood*, Tyndale House Publishers, Carol Stream, IL 2005 speaker Robert Lewis.
6. O'Brien, Brandon, *A Jesus for Real Men*, www.christianityto-day.com/ct/2008/ April/27.48.html, Christianity Today, Carol Stream, Illinois, 2008.
7. Rowland, Helen, www.great-quotes.com/quotes/author/Helen/Rowland, Accessed May 20, 2012
8. Harley, Willard, *His Needs, Her Needs*, Revell-Baker Publishing Group, Grand Rapids, MI, 1986.
9. Lewis, Robert and William Hendricks, *Rocking The Roles*, NavPress, Colorado Springs, CO, 1991.
10. Parker, Kathleen, *Feminism's Devolution; Hoaxers to Harlots*, Orlando Sentinel, Tribune Media Services, Nov 6, 2005.
11. Wolfe, Alan, *The Mystique of Betty Friedan*, Atlantic Monthly: 99.09; Volume 284, No. 3; pages 98-105.
12. Dowd, Maureen, *Are Men Necessary: When Sexes Collide*, Berkley Books, New York, NY, 2005.

13. Smith, Sarah, *Husband Hunting in College: Getting your MRS Degree*, http://www.hercampus.com/career/husband-hunting-college-getting-your-mrs-degree Accessed, May 17, 2012.

14. Davisson, Joel, *The Man of Her Dreams, The Woman of His*, Joel and Kathy, TM, Hilton Head Island, SC, 2004.

15. Thoreau, Henry David. *BrainyQuote.com, Xplore Inc*, 2012. http://brainyquote.com/quotes/quotes/h/henrydavid132662.html, accessed May 20, 2012.

16. Farrell, Warren, *Why Men Earn More: The Startling Truth Behind the Pay Gap—and What Women Can Do About It*, American Management Association, New York, NY, 2005.

17. De Marneffe, Dauphne, *Maternal Desire: On Children, Love, and the Inner Life*, Little Brown & Co, New York, NY, 2004.

18. Jamieson, Fausset, and Brown *Commentary*, Electronic Database. Copyright (c) 1997 by Biblesoft).

19. Gottman, John, *Seven Principles for Making Marriage Work*, Three Rivers Press, New York, NY, 1999.

20. Cohen, Shiri, *The Week Magazine*, March 23, 2012.

21. Ezzo, Gary and Anne Marie Ezzo, *Growing Kids God's Way*, Micah 6:8 Publishing, 1997

22. I saw this presented at a counseling conference in Denver, in 2001, the only place I've ever seen it. I can't remember who the presenter was; I only copied down the notes.

23. Berry, Richard L., *Angry Kids*, Fleming Revell Books, 2001.

24. Rees, Ken, *Millennials use alternative financial services*, USA Today, p 1B, May 17, 2012.

25. Allen, Sara, *Op Ed Piece*, The Denver Post, February, 2005.

26. Flanagan, Caitlin, *To Hell With All That*, Little Brown & Co, New York, NY, 2006.

27. Hirshman, Linda, *Get to Work*, Penguin Group, New York, NY, 2006.

28. Zink, Daniel W., *The Practice of Marriage and Family Counseling and Conservative Christianity, in The Role of Religion in Marriage and Family Counseling* (The Family Therapy and

Counseling Series), ed. J. D. Onedera, New York, NY: Taylor and Francis, 2007.

29. Oswalt, Bill, *Help, I'm Hurting*, Cross Books, Bloomington, IN, 2011.

30. W, Bill, *AA Twelve Steps and Twelve Traditions*, AA World Services Incorporated, New York, NY, 2004.

31. Harvey, Jerry B., *The Abilene Paradox and other Meditations on Management, Organizational Dynamics*, **3** (1): 17-43, 1988.

32. Gothard, Bill, *Institute in Basic Life Principles*, Seminar, www. iblp.org, 2000.

33. Henry, Matthew, *Commentary on the Whole Bible*: New Modern Edition, Electronic Database. Copyright (c) 1991 by Hendrickson Publishers, Inc.

34. Wilcox, W. Bradford, *What's Love Got To Do With It? Equality, Equity, Commitment and Women's Marital Quality*, Social Forces, 84 (3): 1321-1345, March 2006.

35. Littauer, Fred, *Wake Up Men*, Willamette Publishing, Beaverton, OR, 1994.

36. Dillow, James, *Reign of the Servant Kings*, Grace Evangelical Society, Denton, TX, 1992.

37. Wheat, Ed and Gay Wheat, *Intended for Pleasure: Sex Technique and Sexual Fulfillment in Christian Marriage*, Third Edition, Zondervan, Grand Rapids, MI, 1966.

38. Alighieri, Dante, *The Divine Comedy*, New American Library, New York, NY, 2003.

CPSIA information can be obtained at www.ICGtesting.com
Printed in the USA
LVOW13s0036130314

377158LV00002B/118/P